Effective teaching

Effective teaching

A practical guide to improving your teaching

Elizabeth Perrott

Director, International Microteaching Research Unit,
University of Lancaster

Longman
London and New York

Longman Group UK Limited
Longman House, Burnt Mill, Harlow
Essex CM20 2JE, England
and Associated Companies throughout the world.

*Published in the United States of America
by Longman Inc., New York*

First published 1982
Tenth impression 1989

British Library Cataloguing in Publication Data

Perrott, Elizabeth
  Effective teaching.
  1. Teaching
  I. Title
  371.1 '02   LB1025.2

ISBN 0-582-49712-4

Library of Congress Cataloging in Publication Data

Perrott, Elizabeth.
  Effective teaching.

  Bibliography: p.
  Includes index.
  1. Teaching.   I.Title.
LB1025.2.P395   371.1'02   81-20728
ISBN 0–582–49712–4   AACR2

Produced by Longman Singapore Publishers (Pte) Ltd.
Printed in Singapore.

Contents

Acknowledgements

Thanks are due to the University of Lancaster for permission to reproduce Figs. 3.2, 3.3, 7.1, 7.2, 7.3, 7.4, and to E. Beard, University of Keele, for permission to reproduce Figs. 6.1, 6.2, 6.3, 7.5, 7.6, 7.7, 7.8 and 7.9.

We are grateful to the following for permission to reproduce copyright material:

the author, Dr. N. Flanders for our table 8.1 from table 2-1 p 34 (Flanders 1970); Reuters Ltd for the article 'Increase in Birth Rate Goes on' United Nations (NY) Jan 30 1977; Times Newspapers Ltd for extracts from the article 'Tokyo: A City Struggling to Breathe' from *The Times* Nov 25 1970.

Chapter 1

Effective teaching

What is effective teaching?

Some educators claim that good teaching cannot be defined because the criteria differ for every instructional situation and every teacher. They conceive good teaching as being so complex and creative that it defies analysis. There can be no doubt that teaching is a complex task, yet educators usually find it relatively easy to list the characteristics of a good teacher. Although they may differ about the relative importance of these characteristics, rarely do they disagree on the characteristics to be included in such a list.

You might like to make your own list of characteristics to compare with the lists of criteria produced by educational researchers as a result of extensive studies of what teachers do in the classroom.

Observable indicators of effective teaching

Ryan's factors (Table 1.1)

Ryan (1960) and his colleagues conducted a programme of observational studies to identify factors associated with effective teaching. Three main factors emerged from this work. The positive and negative poles of these factors are defined by:

1. Warm and understanding versus cold and aloof.
2. Organized and businesslike versus unplanned and slipshod.
3. Stimulating and imaginative versus dull and routine.

Teachers rated nearer the positive poles of each factor are considered more 'effective' than teachers rated nearer the negative poles.

1

Flanders' indicators (Table 1.1)

Another set of research studies on teacher effectiveness was carried out by Flanders (1970) and his associates. Flanders' studies observe two contrasting styles of teaching: direct and indirect. Direct teaching is characterized by teacher reliance on lecture, criticism, justification of authority and the giving of directions. Indirect teaching is characterized by teacher reliance on asking questions, accepting pupils' feelings, acknowledging pupils' ideas and giving praise and encouragement. A substantial number of studies have found that pupils of 'indirect' teachers learn more and have better attitudes toward learning than pupils of 'direct' teachers. But Flanders suggests that both direct and indirect behaviours are necessary in good teaching, e.g. a teacher can promote learning by a direct teaching strategy such as lecture – explanation to clarify a difficult topic, but the lecture – explanation can be made more indirect by the occasional asking of questions to determine whether pupils understand the presentation.

Rosenshine and Furst's correlates (Table 1.1)

Other researchers have studied teacher characteristics other than direct and indirect teaching. The usual design of these studies is to observe various aspects of teachers' classroom behaviour, and in addition to test the pupils of these teachers at intervals during the school year. Standardized achievement tests are frequently used for this purpose. Pupils' scores before and after a period of instruction (e.g. beginning and end of a school year) are compared to obtain a measure of 'achievement gain'. Finally the data are analysed to determine which teacher behaviour is associated with pupil achievement gains.

Rosenshine and Furst (1973) have written a useful review of these research studies and have identified five teacher characteristics consistently associated with gains in pupils' achievement. The first two characteristics are teacher enthusiasm and businesslike orientation, characteristics also identified in Ryan's research. The third characteristic is teacher clarity. Researchers have measured clarity – or lack of it – in various ways, for example: the amount of time the teacher uses to answer pupils' questions requesting clarification of what the teacher has said; the frequency with which pupils respond to teacher's questions without the teacher having to intersperse additional information or questions; the avoidance of vague words (e.g. some, many, of course) in the teacher's exposition. The fourth Rosenshine and Furst characteristic is variety in teaching. This characteristic can be estimated by counting the number of different instructional materials, tests and teaching devices used by the teacher. Another indication is the extent to which the teacher varies the cognitive level of classroom discourse. The fifth characteristic is the extent to which the teacher provides opportunities for pupils to learn the curriculum content covered in the achievement tests, or the teacher's ability and preference for classroom activities focused on the kinds of cognitive learning usually measured in achievement tests.

Table 1.1 Observable indicators of effective classroom teaching

---

Ryan's factors

1. Teacher is warm and understanding versus cold and aloof
2. Teacher is organized and businesslike versus unplanned and slipshod
3. Teacher is stimulating and imaginative versus dull and routine

---

Flanders indicators of indirect teaching style

1. Teacher asks questions
2. Teacher accepts pupils' feelings
3. Teacher acknowledges pupils' ideas
4. Teacher praises and encourages pupils

Rosenshine and Furst's correlates

1. Teacher is enthusiastic
2. Teacher is businesslike and task oriented
3. Teacher is clear when presenting instructional content
4. Teacher uses a variety of instructional materials and procedures
5. Teacher provides opportunities for pupils to learn the instructional content

---

In recent years researchers have made a concerted effort to identify teaching behaviour that facilitates pupils' learning in specific curriculum areas. Much of this research has focused on reading and mathematics instruction at the primary school level (Bennet 1976).

A large-scale research study conducted in the US by Berliner and Tickenoff (1976), in which modules on the teaching of reading and mathematics at both primary and secondary level were prepared by the researchers and in which teacher effectiveness was measured in terms of pupils' gains on standardized achievement tests, identified twenty-one teachers' behaviours between effective and less effective teachers. However, these lists were found to be surprisingly consistent with the findings of Ryan (1960), Flanders (1970) and Rosenshine (1971).

Observation of the pupils

Observation of the teacher's pupils is also a method of perceiving quality of teaching. Observable indications of effective teaching indicated by pupils' behaviour are given in Table 1.2.

Table 1.2 Observable indications of effective teaching: pupils' behaviour and performance

---

1. Pupils show knowledge and understanding, skills and attitudes intended by the curriculum as measured by performance on tests
2. Pupils exhibit independent behaviour in learning curriculum content
3. Pupils exhibit behaviour which indicates a positive attitude towards teacher and peers
4. Pupils exhibit behaviour which indicates a positive attitude towards the curriculum and the school
5. Pupils exhibit behaviour which indicates a positive attitude towards themselves as learners
6. Pupils do not exhibit behaviour problems in class
7. Pupils seem actively engaged in learning academically relevant material while the class is in session

---

Rosenshine and Berliner (1978) in a review of recent research on teaching, have concluded that this last indicator, which they describe as *academic engaged time*, is an important factor in school achievement. By *academic engaged time*, Rosenshine and Berliner mean the amount of time the pupil spends on reading, writing or other activities which involve the pupil in learning academically relevant material. In other words, the more time, the more achievement. Time spent on other activities was negatively associated with the pupil's achievement. In Chapter 8 the 'at task' technique is described, the use of which can give a good observational measure of this important factor in the pupil's learning.

Observational studies of teaching suggest that the effective teacher is one who is able to demonstrate the ability to bring about intended learning goals, the two critical dimensions of effective teaching being *intent* and *achievement*. Without intent, the pupil's achievements become random and accidental rather than controlled and predictable. However, intent is not enough by itself. Without achievement of his intended learning goals, the teacher cannot truly be called effective. In order to be effective in bringing about intended learning outcomes B. O. Smith (1969) has suggested that a teacher should be prepared in four areas of knowledge:

1. Command of theoretical knowledge about learning and human behaviour.
2. Display of attitudes that foster learning and genuine human relationships.
3. Command of knowledge in the subject-matter to be taught.
4. Control of technical skills of teaching that facilitate pupils' learning.

The teacher as decision-maker

Although these four areas of teacher competence are the basic components of many well-designed teacher education programmes, they do not provide guidelines on what a teacher actually does when teaching.

Suppose you are a secondary school teacher engaged in a general studies course with sixteen-year-old pupils in which one of the topics is energy and society.

1. First you have to decide what you want your pupils to know about energy and society. For instance, you will probably want them to be able to consider existing resources, the possibility of new sources, energy use, safety and environmental impact and the conservation of energy resources.
2. Then you will have to decide what you will accept as evidence of your pupils' learning. Will they have to make a written or oral presentation? Will you require them to analyse a hypothetical or existing situation or will you require them to complete a test?
3. Planning a strategy designed to obtain the desired pupil learning is the next decision. Will you require some reading? Will you give an introductory talk? Will you show a film or

other audio-visual materials? Will you arrange a visit outside the school? Will you arrange for a class discussion? How much time will you allot to the teaching of this topic?
4. As the work progresses you will have to decide, based on pupil reactions, whether it is necessary to adjust your strategy.
5. Lastly, you will need to evaluate the impact and the results of your teaching. Have the pupils shown interest and that they understand the problems of energy use? If not, what can you do about it? How effective were your teaching strategies?

All these questions require decisions from alternative choices. Although the initial decision to deal with the topic of energy and society may be because it is contained in a required syllabus, the teacher is constantly making decisions with regard to pupils' learning and the appropriate teaching strategies to employ. In the example of 'energy and society' you will have to decide how your pupils can best learn about this topic. Would a visit to a nearby power-station be a good way of obtaining their interest, or would a film dealing with the problems of energy supply in our society be better?

Suppose that during a class discussion you pick up cues from some pupils which suggest they have not fully understood the problems involved. Was your teaching strategy ineffective and if so which part needed change or improvement? These decisions are concerned with three basic teaching functions:

1. *Planning.*
2. *Implementation.*
3. *Evaluation.*

Planning

The planning function requires the teacher to make decisions about the pupils' needs, the most appropriate goals and objectives to help meet those needs, the motivation necessary to attain their goals and objectives and the most appropriate teaching strategies for the attainment of those goals and objectives. The planning function usually occurs when the teacher is alone and has time to consider long-term and short-term plans: the pupils' progress; the availability of resources, equipment and materials; the time requirements of particular activities and other issues (Perrott et al. 1977).

Some teaching skills which support this planning function are diagnosing pupil needs, setting goals and objectives and determining appropriate learning activities related to the objectives.

Implementation

The implementation function requires the teacher to implement the decisions made at the planning stage, especially those related to teaching methods, strategies and learning activities. The implementation function occurs when the teacher is interacting with pupils. Teaching skills which support the implementation function include presenting, explaining, listening, introducing, demonstrating, eliciting responses and achieving closure.

Evaluation

The evaluation function requires decisions about the suitability of objectives and the teaching strategies linked to them, and eventually whether or not the pupils are achieving what the teacher intended.

Teaching skills which support this function include specifying the learning objectives to be evaluated; describing the information needed to make such an evaluation; obtaining, recording, analysing and recording that information and forming judgements. In other words, you examine carefully the results of your teaching and decide how well you handled each teaching function. On the basis of this feedback you decide on whether or not to make new plans or try different implementation strategies. In this way your decision-making will become more accurate. Although this model of the teacher as decision-maker is a simplification of what actually occurs in teaching, it is useful at this stage to help the student teacher see the wood without being confused by the trees.

This particular model represents a theory of teaching and makes several basic assumptions. It assumes:

1. that teaching is goal directed, i.e. that some change in pupils' thinking or behaviour is sought;
2. that teachers are active shapers of their own behaviour. They make plans, implement them and continually adjust to new information concerning the effects of their actions;
3. that teaching is a rational process which can be improved by examining its components in an analytical manner;
4. that teaching behaviour can affect pupils' behaviour and learning.

The four areas of teacher competence identified by Smith (1969) represent the broad categories of preparation that teachers need in order to make effective decisions. Competence in theoretical knowledge about learning, attitudes which foster learning and positive relationships, knowledge of the subject-matter to be taught and a repertoire of teaching skills and techniques provide teachers with the tools necessary to make and implement professional decisions.

Earlier in this chapter a variety of general teacher characteristics that can be assessed by observing the teacher's classroom performance were described. It is also possible to observe the teacher's use of more specific strategies and techniques. Discussion, lecture, inquiry, independent learning contracts, simulations and role-playing are examples of teaching strategies that competent teachers might be expected to have in their repertoire. Research has demonstrated the effectiveness of these teaching strategies (Gage 1976), although the evidence is not always conclusive.

Each teaching strategy can be analysed further into a set of techniques. For example, some techniques desirable in class discussion are:

(a) asking higher cognitive questions rather than knowledge-level questions exclusively;
(b) pausing after asking a question to allow pupils time to think;
(c) asking follow-up questions to help pupils improve their original response to a question;
(d) distributing participation evenly among pupils.

Teachers can be observed and rated on their overall effectiveness in using this strategy and also on their effectiveness in using each of the teaching skills involved (Perrott et al. 1975a).

How are teaching skills acquired?

Teaching skills are not acquired without study and diligent practice. This book is designed to start you thinking about teaching skills, to help you understand their purpose and to assist you in practising their application in either simulated or classroom situations.

Acquiring teaching skills is a three-stage process (Fig. 1.1).

The first stage is a *cognitive* one. You will need to study and observe the skill, know the purpose of using it and how it will

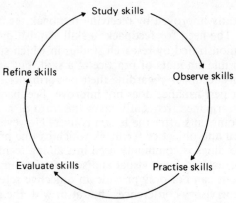

Fig. 1.1   Stages in skill acquisition.

benefit your teaching. This stage will help you to isolate the various elements of the skill, their sequencing and the nature of the final performance. In other words, you will form a concept of the skill.

The second stage is *practice*. Complex skills cannot be learned without a great deal of practice. For example, the seemingly effortless performance of the concert pianist is not achieved without the mastery and flexible use of a set of skills or techniques requiring countless hours of practice, not only of the set pieces he will perform, but also of scales. Similarly, the flexible use of teaching skills in the variety of combinations required by different classroom situations cannot be learned without practice.

However, practising skills in a real classroom after study is analogous to reading a manual on how to operate a motor car and then taking it out into heavy traffic. Obviously, it is best to practise the various elements in simulated or controlled conditions before taking the motor car on to the road. Likewise, the use of training techniques such as *microteaching* (Allen and Ryan 1969) allow the student teacher to practise specific teaching skills under controlled conditions. In this case the controlled conditions involve a short practice period (5–10 minutes), a small class (4–7 pupils), and the practice of a single skill (Perrott 1977).

The third stage in acquiring a teaching skill is to obtain knowledge of results or feedback, which involves evaluation.

Practice is greatly improved by receiving feedback regarding a performance. The need for feedback in skill acquisition has been repeatedly demonstrated by research studies in which subjects are given considerable amounts of practice in a skill, but are deprived of any feedback regarding their performance. Without feedback their performance does not improve. Feedback on a classroom performance frequently takes the form of a supervisor's comments after the lesson is over. However, the immediate, full and objective feedback which can be provided by videotape recordings is commonly used in training techniques such as microteaching. Such visual and sound recordings of teaching sessions can not only provide an objective reference for subsequent supervisory conferences, but also, with the aid of evaluation instruments provided by some training materials (Perrott et al. 1975b), provide for self-evaluation. Audio-recording can also provide useful data for subsequent evaluation either alone or with a supervisor (Perrott 1977), when using training techniques such as microteaching.

Because teacher education has lacked training materials to develop basic teaching skills, teachers in training have traditionally been asked to move from the theoretical model to classroom practice. In such a situation the model becomes subordinate to the practical exigencies of the classroom.

Self-contained model-based training materials which are intended to be inserted between theoretical studies and classroom practice are described in this book. Although, ultimately, teaching skills must be exercised with pupils in real teaching situations, your probability of success will be greatly increased if you first develop a thorough understanding of certain teaching skills; if you arrange controlled practice situations which are reality based; and if you receive feedback so that you might adjust your teaching when necessary.

The purpose of this book is to help you to develop competence in selected teaching skills which are basic to the decision-making model of teaching.

Additional reading

Amidon, A. and Hunter, E. (1966) *Improving Teaching*, Holt, Rinehart and Winston, New York (especially Ch. 5 and 6).

Dunkin, M. J. and Biddle, B. J. (1974) *The Study of Teaching*, Holt, Rinehart and Winston, New York and London (especially Ch. 2).

Miller, G. A. (1970) *The Psychology of Communication*, Pelican, Harmondsworth. This book takes the form of a collection of essays which give a useful general introduction.

Morrison, A. and McIntyre, D. (1973) *Teachers and Teaching*, 2nd edn, Penguin, Harmondsworth (especially Ch. 1 and 5).

Perrott, E. (1977) *Microteaching in Higher Education: Research, Development and Practice*, Society for Research into Higher Education. Monograph, University of Surrey, Guildford, Surrey (especially Ch. 1).

Chapter 2

Planning

Planning is a vital element in teaching, since the whole decision-making model is based on this skill.

Cognitive learning theorists recognize that the amount and rate of learning is influenced by the nature of the subject-matter itself, the way it is broken down and the order in which it is presented (Anderson and Ausubel 1965).

Ausubel (1965), Bruner (1960) and Gagné (1965) agree that control over learning can be exercised most effectively in three ways:

1. Substantively, by showing concern for the structure of a body of subject-matter.
2. Pragmatically, by employing suitable principles of ordering the sequence of subject-matter and constructing its internal logic and organization.
3. Arranging appropriate practice trials.

Specific steps in planning

The basic planning process involves:

1. Choosing the subject-matter of the lesson.
2. Finding out what the pupils already know about the subject you have chosen.
3. Specifying instructional objectives.
4. Devising instructional procedures which will help you to achieve the objectives.
5. Determining how to tell whether or not these procedures work.

Teachers seldom begin planning a lesson in a vacuum. They usually have a course syllabus which is laid down by the school or an external examining body.

Objectives

Having decided on the subject-matter of the lesson you must decide what kinds of things you want your pupils to learn. It is only after the formation of precise goals or specific *instructional objectives* that efficient learning can occur.

Sometimes you may be working from a course syllabus which clearly states its objectives. However, course objectives usually present long-term goals rather than the specific short-term goals which will make good *instructional objectives* for a lesson. However the general aims of the course as a whole usually reflect the values involved in the choice of subject-matter and are an excellent source for affective objectives concerned with attitudes towards subject-matter.

The course aims or objectives are also usually a part of a larger set of goals, e.g. the objectives for fourth form mathematics are seen against the objectives for the mathematics curriculum of the entire school. Seeing your *instructional objectives* as part of a much larger set of objectives should help you understand what to expect from your pupils when they enter the class at the beginning of a session.

The second advantage of objectives found in a course syllabus is that they are not usually tied to particular instructional materials. This leaves you free to choose appropriate materials and procedures to help you to achieve the short-term or *instructional objectives* for your lesson.

Stating instructional objectives

An instructional objective should state what you expect the pupils to learn as a result of your lesson and should describe how the pupils will show what they have learned. In other words, *instructional objectives* place emphasis on what the pupil will do, not upon what the teacher will do; they also indicate how learning is to be observed or evaluated.

For example, it is inadequate simply to state as your *instructional objectives*: 'Pupils will learn about locomotion in aquatic animals.' Although this states a desired learning outcome, it does not indicate how learning is to be observed or evaluated. On the other hand, it is also inadequate to state the objective in terms of a pupil's activity. For example: 'Given six aquatic animals, the pupils will work in groups observing them.' Although this may be a worthwhile activity for the pupils and may lead them to some outcome it is not the outcome itself. What is needed is a pupil-oriented learning outcome such as the following, e.g.: 'Given six different aquatic animals to observe, pupils will report on the methods of locomotion they employ.' This not only describes what the pupil will do, but also the conditions under which the learning will occur, so that the expected behaviour can be observed and evaluated.

Whenever you have an objective stated as a learning activity instead of a learning outcome you can convert it into an acceptable objective simply by answering the following question: 'What will this activity help the pupil to be able to do?' Remember also that many good learning activities are *potentially* useful for helping pupils reach any one of a number of learning outcomes. Consequently, it is important that you should specify precisely what it is you want your pupils to learn from any given activity, and pupils should be told what is expected of them on completion. Learning outcomes are tied to learning focus (selective perception), which in turn is tied to specified goals and objectives.

Suppose, for example, that a teacher's lesson plan includes a class discussion about the effect of inflation on the economy. The pupils as a result might be expected to do any one of the following:

(a) to be able to describe in 1000 words the effect of inflation on the economy;
(b) to be able to define inflation;
(c) to be able to cite examples (from newspaper accounts) of the effect of inflation on the economy.

Whenever the performance expected of pupils is not clearly stated, the problem lies in the verb selected to describe that performance.

When selecting an *instructional objective* for use in your teaching, use a verb which describes observable actions or actions which have observable products, such as to identify, to choose, to solve, to analyse, to explain. Avoid vague unobservable verbs such as, to know, to believe, to appreciate.

There are many processes which cannot be directly observed, e.g. it is not possible to observe the thinking process of a pupil when he is solving a mathematical problem, but the teacher can examine the steps taken to arrive at the solution which will give an indication of the thinking processes involved.

When using active observable verbs to frame objectives, also make the objects of these verbs describe observable end-products. If the object of any of these verbs does not describe an observable end-product, the resulting objective becomes vague and unobservable, e.g.: 'To explain the Middle East Crisis.' What is to be explained, the causes of the Middle East Crisis or the political ideologies involved? Here the problem is not the verb, but the object. Make sure that both the verbs and object are clearly defined, pointing to observable end-products.

Exercise 2.1

From the list of objectives given below, identify those which meet the criterion 'observable' by placing a tally in the appropriate column.

Objectives	Observable	Unobservable
1. To translate a paragraph from a French text		
2. To understand Darwin's theory		
3. To identify four common trees		
4. To describe the characteristics of mammals		
5. To appreciate the 'Moonlight' Sonata		
6. To study a diagram of the circulation in man		

Exercise 2.2

Correct each of the following objectives by making sure both verbs and object clearly define observable actions and end-products.

1. To learn this week's French vocabulary.
2. To know the rules for correct punctuation.
3. To know the causes of the Civil War.
4. To understand the difference between hard- and softwoods.
5. To know Chapter 3 in your chemistry book.

Answer key

Suggested corrections are given below. Other corrections are possible, but carefully check that verbs describe observable action or end-products of that action.

1. (a) To write the English equivalent of each French word in this week's vocabulary.
   (b) To use each word in this week's French vocabulary in a conversation with the teacher.
2. (a) To state the rules for correct punctuation.
   (b) To punctuate a paragraph correctly.
   (c) To correct incorrect punctuation in a given passage.
   (d) To explain each punctuation rule and write a sentence illustrating the proper application of each rule.
3. (a) To list the causes of the Civil War.
   (b) To arrange the events causing (leading up to the beginning of) the Civil War in sequential order.
4. (a) To distinguish between the hard- and softwoods in a number of given samples.
   (b) Explain the difference between hard- and softwoods.
   (c) Give six examples of trees having hardwood and six examples of softwoods.
5. (a) To recall the major facts in Chapter 3 and list them from memory.
   (b) To explain the contents of Chapter 3 to the teacher, using your own words.

Exercise 2.3

Each of the following objectives is poorly written. (a) Identify the major problem and (b) rewrite the objective to correct that problem.

1. To show the class how to extract moisture from soil.
2. To understand the problems of developing countries.
3. To grasp the significance of the energy crisis.
4. To collect newspaper clippings about the European Economic Community (EEC).
5. To view a film on air pollution.

Answer key

1. (a) *Problem:* Teacher-focused learning activity.
   (b) *Correction:* To investigate the amount of moisture in soil. Pupils, working in groups of two, will carry out an experiment to measure the moisture contained in 100 grams of soil.
2. (a) *Problem:* Vague, unobservable.
   (b) *Correction:* To describe the problems of one developing country and discuss with the pupils possible solutions to

these problems.
3. (a) *Problem:* Vague, unobservable.
   (b) *Correction:* To consider the sources and uses of energy.
       To discuss the pros and cons of the use of nuclear energy.
4. (a) *Problem:* Learning *activity* rather than outcome.
   (b) *Correction:* To list the advantages and disadvantages of
       EEC membership.
5. (a) *Problem:* Learning *activity* rather than outcome.
   (b) *Correction:* To explain in your own words the necessity
       for control of air pollution giving examples to support
       your argument.

Lesson plans

Making a lesson plan involves:

1. Deciding on the kind of things you want the pupils to learn
   and stating what is to be learned in terms of precise
   instructional objectives.
2. Specifying an appropriate sequence of topics and tasks.
3. Describing the teaching methods to be used to move pupils
   towards the learning objective.
4. Describing how the pupils will demonstrate what they have
   learned or determining how to tell whether or not the
   procedures have worked by establishing checkpoints to
   provide feedback and monitor pupils' progress.

Remember that without a plan which features objectives, an
observer is likely to misjudge the effectiveness of your classroom
behaviour, e.g. a class discussion which contains too many recall
questions on the part of the teacher is likely to be criticized
unless the reason for doing so is explained. If the recall questions
are intended to be used as a device to reinforce the information
contained in a lesson which the class found difficult and are
followed by a discussion in which the class are encouraged to
reflect on and apply the information they have gained, it could
be an effective strategy. But without your objectives and the
strategy used to achieve them being described your teaching
performance may be misjudged. Knowledge of your plans and
intent enables the supervisor to help the student analyse how well
classroom behaviour corresponded to what was planned.

A guide to making a suitable lesson plan is given below.

Lesson planning guide

1. General headings of date, class, age of pupils, number in class, duration of lesson and subject taught.
2. General aim: Why am I teaching this?
3. Particular aim or instructional objective: Exactly what do I hope the pupils will learn as a result of this lesson?
4. Subject-matter: What am I teaching?
5. The intended structure of the lesson and how the time will be used. The form of this section will vary according to the kind of work undertaken. It should indicate:
   (a) the teacher's work: e.g. exposition, questioning; showing of film or filmstrip; individual coaching – explaining, where possible, the kind of help it is hoped to give.
   (b) the pupil's work: e.g. their share in planning and carrying through the work; discussion; completion of exercises or questionnaires; individual or group work.
   (c) where possible, the order in which the work is expected to progress, e.g. accompanying diagrams might show planned blackboard work and use of other visual aids, samples of exercises set, assignments, etc.
6. Materials and equipment: (a) required by teacher, (b) required by pupils.
7. Subsequent comments (to be completed as soon as possible after the lesson is over):
   (a) How far the work has developed as planned.
   (b) Particularly good aspects of the work: e.g. things in which the children showed unusual interest; marked cooperation on the part of the children; particularly useful material or equipment; outstandingly good work.
   (c) Particularly bad aspects of the work: e.g. things in which the children showed very little interest; behaviour difficulties; inadequate provision of material or equipment; unforeseen difficulties; outstandingly bad work.
   (d) Assessment of the total situation, suggestions about future work, good points to be followed up, deficiencies made good, desirable modifications in original programme.

Teaching activities or methods

It is important to remember that teaching and learning are two different functions, the process of teaching being carried out by one person, while the process of learning is carried out by another. If teaching–learning processes are to work effectively there must be some connection or bridge between the teacher and the learner. Much of this book, therefore, deals with the *communication skills* required by teachers to become effective in making these connections. These skills primarily involve talking.

Research studies have shown that the average teacher does 70 per cent of the talking in primary and secondary classrooms (Flanders 1970; Perrott 1977). The percentage is probably higher in some settings (e.g higher education) and lower in others. Much of this time is spent in presenting new concepts and information to pupils using narration, description and explanation. This activity, which may be called the lecture–explanation method, is teacher centred, interaction between teacher and pupils being minimal.

Lecture and explanation techniques

In almost all lessons or learning sequences the teacher has to present information and ideas. He has to introduce topics, summarize the main points of the learning activity and stimulate further learning. All these activities require the use of lecture–explanation techniques at various points in a learning sequence, but they must not take up too much of the lesson time.

A rough guide is that lecture–explanation, without any pupil participation, should not usually exceed 10–20 per cent of the lesson time, the time being nearer 10 per cent for younger pupils and 20 per cent for older pupils. However, teachers frequently use techniques which ensure that pupils do not sit passively through an entire lecture–explanation sequence. Asking pupils questions about the lesson is an example of a technique designed to create pupil involvement.

Discussion

Discussion consists of questions, answers and comment by both teacher and pupils. Since it involves feedback and pupil participation one would expect it to be an effective method of learning. This expectation is borne out by research evidence (McKeachie 1963; Abercrombie 1971). It is a useful preliminary or follow-up to any independent learning and it is useful in helping pupils to work out complicated problems. Most lessons should contain some discussion.

Independent studies

These methods vary from the common situation in which each pupil carries out a given activity independently, for example the solving of a mathematics problem or the translation of a passage into another language, at one end of the continuum, to a completely open-ended choice of individual activity at the other, e.g. an 'activity' session in a primary classroom in which objectives are hidden until the tasks are complete. In between these two are the inquiry methods commonly used by science teachers in which specific problems are set for investigation, bearing in mind the resources available, but freedom in the methods of solving the problem are allowed. Inquiry methods although often effective can be time-consuming, requiring decisions by the teacher on the best mix of methods to use to achieve his instructional objectives. The use of these methods require very careful planning in advance on the part of the teacher (Perrott et al. 1977), requiring as they do arrangements for independent study by individuals or small groups.

Gage and Berliner (1975) describe the most common teaching methods as being a combination of lecture–explanation, discussion and individual instruction. In the following chapters, we shall consider in greater detail the teaching skills which play an important role in these three common teaching strategies.

Additional reading

For a comprehensive guide on teaching conduct: **Peterson, A. D. C.** (1966) *The Techniques of Teaching*, Vol. 1 *Primary*, Vol. 2 *Secondary*, Pergamon Press, London. On writing instructional objectives: **Mager, R. F.** (1962) *Preparing Instructional Objectives*, Fearon Press, Palo Alto, California; **Popham, W. J. et al.** (1969) *Instructional Objectives*, Rand McNally, London.

Chapter 3

Lesson presentation skills

Lessons which combine lecture–explanation, discussion and individual instruction require a considerable amount of verbal structuring and directing to keep classroom activities progressing smoothly. In other words the teacher assumes a role similar to that of a presenter of a radio or television programme. Regardless of the level of the pupils, the necessity of exposing pupils to new facts, concepts and principles; of explaining difficult ideas; of clarifying issues or of exploring relationships more often than not places the teacher in a position where he has to do a great deal of presenting. In order to become an effective presenter there are five skills which it is important to master. These are:

1. Set induction.
2. Closure.
3. Stimulus variation.
4. Clarity of explanation.
5. Use of examples.

Set induction

The concept of pre-instructional procedure or set comes from research on learning. This research appears to indicate that the activities which precede a learning task have an influence upon the outcome of that task and that some instructional sets promote learning better than others.

The functions of set induction

The functions of set induction are as follows:

1. To focus the student's attention on what is to be learned by

gaining their interest, e.g. the teacher begins a lesson on movement in aquatic animals by introducing an aquarium containing a variety of aquatic animals into the classroom.

2. Transition set.
   A common type of set provides a smooth transition from known or already covered material to new or unknown material. This is often achieved by a question-and-answer session on the topic covered in the last lesson, providing a linkage with the next topic. Alternatively, it may use examples from pupils' general knowledge to move to new material by use of example or analogies.

3. To provide a structure or framework for the lesson.
   Research studies indicate that teachers can influence pupils' behaviour best when they are told in advance what is expected of them. DeCecco (1968) calls this 'the expectancy function of teachers', while Gage and Berliner (1975) speak of *advance organizers*. Set should attempt to create an organizing framework for the body of the lesson, e.g. supposing you wish your pupils to make detailed observations of movement in aquatic animals, to say, 'I want you all to observe the animals in the aquarium', is not only a weak set but will probably cause disruption in your classroom while all the pupils try to crowd round the aquarium. To improve your set you might extend it by saying, 'We shall be studying movement in three different aquatic animals during this lesson. First of all I shall ask you to examine one of these animals in the glass dish which will be provided for each of you and to observe its movements.'
   A sufficient set is one which gives adequate preparation so that while engaged on a learning activity the pupil is able to come near to your instructional objectives.

4. To give meaning to a new concept or principle.
   The introduction to an activity can also contain guides or cues which will be helpful to the pupils in understanding the lesson. For instance, appropriate use of examples and analogues can help pupils to understand abstract ideas, e.g. to begin a lesson on the principles of classification in living organisms by introducing a variety of common plants and animals into the classroom for the pupils to categorize.

Set induction is not used only at the beginning of a lesson. It

may also be appropriately used during the course of a lesson.
Examples of activities for which set induction is appropriate:
to begin a new unit of work
to initiate a discussion
to introduce an assignment
to prepare for a field excursion
to prepare for a practical session in the laboratory
to prepare for viewing a film or TV programme
to introduce a guest speaker

Exercise 3.1

During school practice periods you will have the opportunity to observe
lessons. Take this opportunity to note the pre-instructional procedures
used by placing a tally opposite the appropriate category in the guide.

Appraisal guide: Pre-instructional procedures set

---

1. The teacher's method of introducing the lesson
   focused on the topic and engaged the pupils' interest.

---

2. The teacher's introduction provided a smooth
   transition from known material to new material.

---

3. The introduction created an organizing framework for
   the lesson.

---

4. The teacher gave cues or used materials which helped
   the pupils to understand the ideas explored in the
   body of the lesson.

Exercise 3.2

Now take the opportunity to practise the skill of set induction yourself.
Plan a short microlesson (Ch.1, p. 9) of five or ten minutes length
concentrating on the introduction and arrange to give it to five or six
pupils, or a few of your fellow students.
   During a teaching practice period you might arrange to do this with
some volunteer pupils during the lunch break or by offering to take on
some small-group work for your supervising teacher. If you decide to
work with some of your fellow students you could make this a part of
your lesson preparation. In either case arrange for some objective
feedback. This can be most easily arranged by using an audio-recorder.

This will allow you to listen to yourself immediately after the lesson is over and to use the appraisal guide to classify your own performance. If you have been working with some of your fellow students, you might ask them to complete the appraisal guide too and then compare notes.

It is also a good plan to follow the analysis of feedback by another attempt at the lesson and then evaluate it for improvement. The employment of this teach-reteach cycle allows you to put into practice what you have learned from feedback from your first attempt. If opportunity allows, you could also obtain feedback by means of a video-recorder. This would also give you valuable information about your non-verbal behaviour.

This type of practice makes it easier to concentrate on specific teaching skills than with the full class, because you are dealing only with a small group of pupils for a short time, and are receiving immediate feedback. Microteaching is a simple way to practise teaching skills in a situation of manageable proportions, and obtain objective feedback for analysis. It is analogous to the practice of scales on the piano before attempting to play a melody. (Fig. 3.1)

Fig. 3.1 A microlesson in progress.

Video- and audio-recording

Video- and audio-recordings will allow you to see or hear yourself as pupils see or hear you. Fortunately video- and audio-recorders are becoming increasingly accessible. Until relatively recently they were both expensive and bulky. Their cost, especially the cost of audio-recorders, is usually within reach of colleges and schools, and indeed you may possess your own audio-recorder.

Teachers almost invariably find that both audio- and video-recordings provide important, self-learning experiences. Our experience indicates that teachers when first exposed to video-recordings of themselves, tend to focus on the 'cosmetics' of their performance (e.g. physical appearance, clothes, voice quality). This is a natural reaction. But with continual exposure to this type of feedback the teacher becomes accustomed to his recorded image and is able to concentrate on those aspects of behaviour he is practising (Perrott et al. 1975a). This is especially the case where self-appraisal guides are used and the teacher is free to erase his recording after appraisal. (Fig. 3.2)

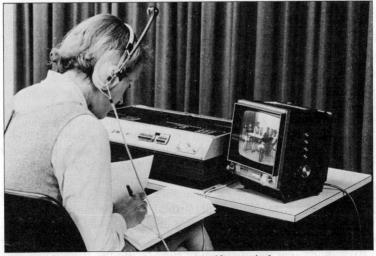

Fig. 3.2   Evaluation of microlesson – self-appraisal.

Recording equipment

Suitable video equipment for microteaching is a portable camera kit containing camera (with wide-angle lens), viewfinder, tripod and omnidirectional microphone, a video-cassette recorder, video-monitor for playback and a video-cassette. This equipment can be set up in a normal classroom and additional lighting is not normally required. (Fig. 3.3) If a free room can be

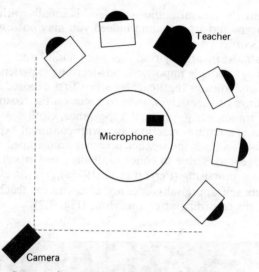

Fig. 3.3 Suggested arrangement for microteaching.

found the equipment can be both set up and stored there, microteaching groups being taken along to this room as opportunities present themselves. Viewing of recordings can also be made there.

Audio-recorders are more readily portable, many models having built-in microphones and being powered by batteries. The recording process becomes more complicated as the size of the group increases. It is far easier to record a group of five pupils than a group of thirty pupils, as most microphones have a small pick-up range. Therefore microteaching does not usually present recording problems. With larger groups place the microphone near the teacher, so that you record everything the teacher says, even if you are able to record only some of what the pupils say.

Remember that the appraisal of long recordings is a very time-consuming occupation. A ten-minute microlesson is usually quite long enough. If longer recordings are made it is often more feasible to use a sampling technique, selecting five-minute segments from beginning, middle or end as appropriate.

Closure

Closure is a complement of set induction. It draws attention to the end of a specific learning sequence, or of an entire lesson by focusing attention on what has been learned.

It needs to be carefully planned, and for this the teacher needs to watch the clock, allowing adequate time to initiate closure before the lesson is due to end. The careful timing of the learning activities in a lesson plan will be of assistance here. To be overtaken by the bell is a most ineffective end to a lesson.

Effective closure reinforces what has been learned by reviewing the key points of a lesson and relating them to other material the pupils have already learned.

The functions of closure

The objective of closure is to help the pupils retain the important points presented in the lesson, thus increasing the possibility that they will be able to recall and use that information at another time.

Closure is sometimes used during the course of a lesson, e.g.:

(a) to end a discussion by calling on a pupil or pupils to summarize the major points covered;
(b) to end a laboratory exercise by calling on different pupils to list the steps carried out, the results obtained and the conclusions drawn;
(c) to follow up a film, TV programme, guest speaker, by a discussion of the main points made with a view to reinforcement;
(d) to follow up a homework assignment reviewed in class by using praise and encouragement, e.g. 'that was a difficult assignment. I am pleased with the way you tackled it.' This is social closure in contrast to other forms of closure which are cognitive. It is important in giving the pupils a sense of achievement and is particularly useful when used in referring to a difficult learning task.

Exercise 3.3

Use the appraisal guide given below to analyse the closure techniques used in the lessons you observe.

Appraisal guide: Closure

---

1. The teacher summarized the main points of the lesson at the end.

---

2. The teacher had the pupils summarize the main points of the lesson by questioning at the end.

---

3. The teacher consolidated major points and ideas during the lesson before moving on to new topics.

---

4. The encouragement and praise given by the teacher created a sense of achievement.

Exercise 3.4

Prepare a microlesson lasting ten minutes in which you practise the skill of closure. Arrange for an audio-recording to be made. Listen to the playback and record instances of closure techniques by placing a tally opposite the apropriate category on the appraisal guide.

Varying the stimulus

The purpose of this skill is to arouse pupils' attention to focus it upon the content of the lesson. While the most effective way of doing this is to make the content itself interesting, this is not sufficient by itself. An interesting subject can be made tedious by the manner in which it is presented. Rosenshine's review (1970) of studies of teachers' enthusiasm and pupil's achievement gives clear evidence that animated behaviour on the part of the teacher stimulates the attending behaviour of pupils and enhances learning. This skill of *varying the stimulus* (Allen, Fortune and Cooper, 1968), is based on learning theory which indicates that uniformity of the perceived environment tends to lead people into mental inactivity, while changes in the perceived environment attract their attention and stimulate mental activity.

It is of course possible for some changes in the environment to distract attention away from the content of a lesson, so it is important that the ways in which teachers vary the stimuli should focus pupils' attention on lesson objectives.

Stimulus variation refers to those teacher actions, sometimes planned and sometimes spontaneous, that develop and maintain a high level of attention on the part of the pupils, during the course of a lesson.

Stimulus variation techniques

Teacher movements

Teacher movements can have an important effect on pupils' behaviour, e.g. the physical shift from one part of the room to the other causes pupils' attention to be focused directly on the teacher during presentation. However, remember that random nervous movements, such as pacing up and down can irritate and interrupt rather than improve communication.

Focusing behaviours

The use of focusing to enhance communication is well documented. Focusing is the teachers' way of intentionally directing pupils' attention. This control is mainly accomplished by the use of either verbal statements, specific gestures or movements, or some combination of the two.

(a) *Verbal focusing* involves emphasis of particular words, statements or directions, e.g. 'Listen to this', 'Look at this diagram', 'Watch what happens when I add this liquid to the solution', 'Observe the way in which the animal moves'.

(b) *Gestural focusing* consists chiefly of eye movements, facial expressions and movements of head, arms and body (Argyle 1970). Gestures are important means of communication between teacher and pupil. They are used to (i) gain attention, (ii) to indicate emotions.
   (i) Gaining attention
       Watch how an experienced teacher maintains eye contact with an entire class. This is important in gaining attention. Other examples of movements which accomplish this aim are using a pointer to indicate an object, turning the body in the direction of an object, clapping the hands to gain attention.
   (ii) Indicating feeling or emotion
       For example smiling, frowning, raising the eyebrows, nodding the head to give encouragement. Alternatively, gesture can be used to qualify verbal cues, e.g. 'Try to answer' said with a glare conveys a different meaning from the same phrase uttered with an encouraging smile.

(c) *Verbal–gestural focusing* combines gestural and verbal focusing. Sometimes this is for emphasis, e.g. teacher points to a diagram and says, 'Look at this diagram.' Teacher uses a pointer on a map to follow the course of a river and says, 'Follow the course of this river.'

Changes in speech pattern

Variations in quality, expressiveness, tone and rate of speech can increase animation, e.g. a change in the teacher's rate, volume or tone of speech can increase the pupil's attention. Planned silence or pausing can also be most effective in capturing attention by contrasting sound with silence. It can create suspense or expectation, e.g. a sudden pause in the middle of a sentence. Three seconds is an adequate length of pause. Nervousness often makes a teacher afraid of silence and anxious to rush to fill any pause with extra questions or statements. Notice that an experienced teacher always pauses after he has asked a question, and if he thinks a pupil can extend an answer he may pause again to prompt the pupil to continue, sometimes combining the pause with a smile and a nod to indicate encouragement.

Changing interactions

Teachers may employ three main types of interaction with a class.

1. Teacher/group interaction
   This is a teacher-centred type of interaction, where the teacher lectures or demonstrates to the class as a whole. Any questions which are asked are directed to the group as a whole rather than to individuals, e.g. the teacher demonstrates a method for extracting chlorophyll from a leaf, so that it may be tested for the presence of starch.

2. Teacher–pupil interaction
   This is a teacher-directed rather than teacher-centred interaction style. In this situation the teacher questions specific pupils by name in order to promote pupil exposition and/or discussion, e.g. pupils have completed a series of lessons on a given topic and the teacher has prepared a series of questions based on this topic which range in difficulty from requiring recall of factual information to those requiring application of knowledge acquired to a new situation.

3. Pupil–pupil interaction
   Some examples of such interactions are:

(a) class discussion in which the teacher plays a management role redirecting pupils' questions to other pupils for comment and clarification, e.g. 'How would you answer John's question Peter?'

(b) A class working in small groups on project work or experimentation which is discussed among themselves. Here again the teacher's role is a management one.

(c) A situation where pupils go to the board to show the steps they used to solve a problem.

(d) Pupils engaged in role-playing or acting.

Shifting sensory channels
During a lesson pupils process information by means of the senses – sight, touch, smell, taste and hearing, and research studies indicate that pupils' ability to process information can be significantly increased by appealing to sight and sound alternatively, e.g. listen/look/listen. A teacher explains verbally and follows this by drawing a diagram on the blackboard on which he questions pupils. Or, look/listen/look. A teacher shows a short film which he follows by a question and answer sequence, and then shows the film again. Listen/look; touch/look; listen. The teacher explains the structure of a feather using a large diagram; then he provides feathers for the pupils to touch, feel and draw; this activity is followed by a group discussion. Touch/listen; the teacher allows pupils to feel three different samples of soil – a clay, a loam and a sandy soil. This is followed by a class discussion and the setting up of apparatus by pupils working in small groups to separate the constituents of a soil. (Here sense shifting is combined with a change of interaction from pupil–pupil to teacher–class to pupil–pupil interaction.)

Exercise 3.5

Choose a topic of interest to your pupils and prepare a microlesson lasting ten minutes. Incorporate into the lesson as many of the ways of varying the stimulus as appropriate. Arrange for a video-recording to be made of it. View it and assign yourself ratings on the appraisal guide given below. Comment on ways in which you think you could have improved your lesson and repeat with a different group. Analyse again, noting any improvements.

If it is not feasible to make a video-recording, make an audio-recording and arrange for a colleague or your supervisor to observe your microlesson and complete the appraisal guide. Listen to the recording and assign yourself ratings on the verbal stimuli used. Discuss the ratings of non-verbal stimuli with your colleague or supervisor.

Summary

Incorporate into your microlesson the following behaviours:

1. Teacher movements.
2. Focusing behaviours
   (a) verbal;
   (b) gestures.
3. Changes in speech pattern.
4. Changing interactions.
5. Shifting sensory channels.
6. Distracting behaviours.

Exercise 3.6

Appraisal guide: Stimulus variation

Record instances of stimulus variation falling into any one of the following categories by placing a tally opposite the appropriate category.

1. *Teacher movements* At various times during the lesson the teacher moved about the teaching space.	
2. *Focusing behaviours* (a) Verbal – emphasis was given by verbal expressions, e.g. 'Watch this', 'Listen carefully'. (b) Gestures – Used gestures to convey extra meaning. Note whether hands, body, head, face.	
3. *Changes in speech pattern* Variation of rate, volume and expressiveness.	
4. *Changing interactions* The teacher varied the kind of pupil participation: teacher/group, teacher/pupil, pupil/pupil.	

5. *Shifting sensory channels* Use of visual material (words on blackboard, objects, pictures, films) in such a way that the pupil must look to obtain the information, not listen. Use of touch. Use of smell. Use of sound other than speech.	

6. *Distracting behaviours*
Unnecessary gestures. Inappropriate movement.
Voice – too loud, too quiet
       – flat
       – too fast, too slow.	

Clarity of explanation

'To explain is to relate an object, event, actions or state of affairs to some other object, event, action or state of affairs; or to show the relation between an event or state of affairs and a principle or generalization; or to show relationships between principles or generalizations' (Bellack et al. 1966).

Giving explanations, however, appears to be much more difficult than making factual reports. A major barrier appears to be lack of clarity in the presentation of explanations. Empirical evidence suggests that *clarity of presentation* is an aspect of behaviour which has considerable influence on the effectiveness of classroom teaching.

Among the factors which are important in contributing to effectiveness in making an explanation are continuity, simplicity and explicitness.

Continuity

1. Sequence of Discourse
The connections between the various points dealt with in a lesson should be made obvious. A lesson may have any one of several different kinds of connecting thread (e.g. deductive, inductive, historical, enumerative), but whatever the connecting thread it should always be clear and apparent. Diversions from a central theme should be minimal, and where such diversions are necessary – most often as a result of pupil participation – it should be made clear that they are diversions, otherwise pupils tend to believe that they do not understand something, because they do not see the relevance of the diversion to the main theme.

33

If a teacher diverges from the main line of his exposition to go off at various tangents, it is difficult for the pupils to know the points upon which their attention should be focused. When observing lessons, look for *discontinuities* in theme, i.e. points at which the teacher changes the topic or line of argument without summarizing the relationship of what has been said to the theme he is now picking up.

2. Fluency

The teacher can also help pupils to understand an explanation by the use of easily intelligible grammatical sentences. The ability to talk coherently appears to depend partly on mastery of the subject-matter and social confidence in the class situation, but is probably most dependent on careful advance planning of one's exposition.

Indications of lack of fluency are the number of times the teacher interrupts himself to reformulate what he is saying and the number of sentences he leaves unfinished.

Continuity is important, not only in discourse but also in questioning. When pupils are asked a question, if they are following the lesson they will attempt to think of an answer. If the teacher provides further information or restates the question differently because he feels his first question lacks precision or is too difficult – he is likely to confuse pupils by dividing their attention between his first question and the new information he is giving them. Ideally, questions should be phrased initially in such a way that it is possible to answer them without additional help. In any case give your pupils time to think and suggest answers. Only if an adequate answer is not forthcoming, should you rephrase your question or give *prompting* information.

Simplicity

1. Avoid a grammatical complexity

Since explanations are concerned with relationships they are often complex. A common cause of failure is the inclusion of too much information in one sentence. Keep sentences short, and if relationships are complex consider communicating them by visual means. By using diagrams, tables and models, relationships which are very difficult to explain through speech alone, can be simplified. When observing lessons note sentence construction. Look out for sentences with more than one qualifying clause. Also note instances of the use of visual means to make relationships clear.

2. *Vocabulary*

The use of specialist terms without explanation or definition of their meaning does not add to the clarity of an explanation. Use simple language within the pupil's normal vocabulary for effective communication, and only introduce specialist terms when they are necessary for mastering an important concept in a subject area. Quite apart from specialist vocabulary, teachers can also limit their success in explaining by using language which is not within the experience of their pupils.

Explicitness

A major reason for failure to explain effectively is the assumption that there is more common ground between the teacher and pupils than in fact exists. Under the circumstances the normal tendency is to be less explicit than one would otherwise be, and to attempt to communicate by relatively vague references. One indication of such vagueness is the frequent use of phrases such as 'of course', 'you know'. The precise characteristics of vague language will depend on the subject being discussed, but a common example is vagueness about size and number, with the use of words such as 'a little', 'some', or 'many', 'small', 'large' in situations where the pupils may make false assumptions as to actual amount or size involved.

1. *The elements of an explanation*

A clear explanation depends upon (i) the identification of the components to be related, e.g. objects, events, processes, generalizations, and (ii) the identification of the relationship between components, e.g. causal, justifying, interpreting, mechanical. This identification of the components and the relationship between them is something which the teacher has to do first for himself. The teacher's failure to do this is a primary cause of a confused presentation.

2. *Explaining statements*

It is quite easy to provide good information about something, with an explanation being *implicit* within this information and yet fail to make the explanation *explicit*. One of the few aspects of teachers' explaining behaviour, which has been clearly shown to be related to pupils' attainment is the extent to which explanations are made *explicit*. A good index of whether this is being done is the frequency of the teacher's use of explaining links. The great majority of sentences, which make explicit a relation between two ideas or processes, use one of the words or phrases given below:

	because	as a result of
	why	therefore
so	so that	in order to
	by	through

Although explanation has been discussed as largely a one-way process of communication, all that has been said applies equally to a questioning mode of teaching or discussion. Remember also that there is always a need to question for feedback on pupil understanding and to be responsive to the feedback thus obtained.

When observing lessons use the appraisal guide given below.

Exercise 3.7

Prepare a microlesson lasting ten minutes in which you explain a difficult concept to a group from one of your classes. Arrange for an audio-recording to be made of it. Replay the recording using the appraisal guide to evaluate your performance.

Appraisal guide: Clarity of explanation

Record instances of behaviour falling into any one of the following categories by putting a tally opposite the appropriate category.

Discontinuities in theme	
Self-interruptions and unfinished sentences	
Questions without chance for pupils to answer	
Grammatically over-complex sentences	
Use of visual techniques for explanation	
Unnecessary technical terms	

Unexplained difficult vocabulary	
Vague words or sentences	
Objects and relations between them identified	
Explaining links	
Comments	

Using examples

The use of examples is basic to teaching and is a skill commonly used in clarifying explanation. Effective teaching of new concepts, relationships or principles depends on the teacher's ability to use examples and seek examples from pupils, in such a way as to help pupils to comprehend these new concepts.

Concepts allow us to organize and store similar pieces of information efficiently. Once formed they eliminate our need to treat each new piece of knowledge as a separate category. Martorella (1972) conceives concepts as hooks on which we hang new experiences. When we confront a sufficiently novel situation for which we have no hooks, we either force the information on to an incompatible hook, or else create a new one. In short, concepts organize our knowledge structure and keep it from becoming unwieldy and dysfunctional.

A useful aspect of concepts lies in their ability to speed up and simplify communication. If teacher and taught share similar concepts, communication is easy, without the need to explain in detail every idea or principle. However, a particular problem for teachers is that the concepts they use in their thinking are often not shared by their pupils who, being less experienced in a particular area of thought, have had neither the opportunity nor the need to develop such general and complex concepts.

It follows that effective teaching of new concepts, relationships and principles depends on the teacher's ability (1) to make use of pupils' existing concepts, and (2) to use relatively concrete information in attempting to communicate relatively abstract ideas. By focusing on phenomena, situations and ideas well within pupils' experience and understanding, the teacher can lead

37

pupils to perceive common features and thus to abstract generalizations. For instance, when it is clear that a statement made to the class is ambiguous or simply not understood, the teacher must clarify it by the use of examples drawn from the pupil's experience and present level of understanding, and in this way lead to the original statement, idea or principle. To ensure that examples are relevant the teacher needs to start by obtaining appropriate information about his pupils.

Inductive and deductive approaches

There are two basic approaches to the use of examples:

1. The inductive approach
   Where you start with examples, and make an inference or generalization upon the basis of those examples.
2. The deductive approach
   Where the generalization is stated first and then applied to a number of examples.

Research has failed to show any general superiority of one approach over the other. It may well be that the effectiveness of the deductive approach may be that the initial statement, even when not understood, focuses the attention of pupils on those aspects of the examples to which the teacher wishes them to attend. On the other hand, the effectiveness of the inductive approach may well be in helping pupils to acquire skills of looking for order in an apparently patternless set of data.

Guidelines for the effective use of examples

1. Start with the simplest examples that will achieve your goal, working from simple examples to more complex examples.
2. Start with examples relevant to the pupils' experience and level of knowledge.
3. The point of using examples is to illustrate, clarify or substantiate a principle, generalization, idea or rule. Therefore, if you use the deductive approach and start with an idea or generalization and then obtain or give examples, it is important then to relate the examples again to the specific idea or generalization you wish to teach. If you have used the inductive approach, and have started with examples from which a generalization is inferred, then it is important to obtain more examples to illustrate and clarify the point. The principle is always to relate your examples to the point which

you are trying to teach, or in other words examples are much more likely to be effective if their relation to the generalization they exemplify is made explicit, rather than being assumed to be obvious.

4. It is important to check to see whether you have taught what you intended to teach. In order to obtain feedback on the understanding of the generalization taught, ask pupils to give examples of the idea which you were trying to teach. Where pupils are unable to provide or recognize examples, or to apply the principle to relevant problems, further clarification is obviously necessary. This may involve using simpler examples or analysing the generalization into several parts, exemplifying each of these separately and then synthesizing a rule or generalization from them.

Summary of guidelines for the effective use of examples
1. Start with simple examples and work towards more complex examples.
2. Start with examples relevant to pupils' experience and level of knowledge.
3. Relate examples to the principle, idea or generalization being taught.
4. Check to see whether you have accomplished your objective by asking the pupils to give you examples which illustrate the point you were trying to make.

Use the appraisal guide given below to analyse the use of examples in the lessons you observe.

Exercise 3.8

1. Prepare a microlesson lasting ten minutes.
2. Arrange for an audio-recording to be made of your microlesson. Use as many examples as you can to clarify a generalization which you intend the pupils to understand.
3. Listen to the recording of your microlesson and tally instances of the behaviour listed below by placing a tick in the appropriate box.

Appraisal guide: Use of examples

Number of instances	1	2	3	4	5	6	7	8	9	10
Explicit statement of generalization by teacher										
Teacher gives example which exemplifies generalization being taught										
Teacher uses examples which are relevant to the pupils' knowledge and experience										
Teacher asks pupils to give an example illustrating the generalization being taught										
The teacher started with simple examples of generalization followed by more complex examples										
Teacher had to give further clarification of generalization by the use of simpler examples										
Comments: Note whether an inductive or deductive approach was used										

Interpretation

Your tally should indicate how effective your teaching has been. If for instance you failed to obtain examples from pupils without further clarification and the use of simpler examples, modify your microlesson in preparation for teaching it to another group of pupils. If you are doubtful about your effectiveness, ask a colleague or your supervisor to code it with you.

Additional reading

Stones, E. and Morris, S. (1972) *Teaching Practice – Problems and Perspectives*, Methuen, London.

Chapter 4

Questions

The important role played by questions in the educational process has been discussed by many educators. In fact it may well be the most important activity in which teachers engage.

Teachers certainly rely on question-asking as a major part of their teaching repertoire. As long ago as 1912 Stevens found that high school teachers ask almost 400 questions during an average school day, and these findings have been reinforced by more recent studies. For instance Floyd (1960) found that a sample of primary school teachers asked an average of 348 questions during each school day; and another by Moyer (1966) showed that teachers asked an average of 180 questions during each science lesson. At high-school level Bellack et al. (1966) found that 'the core of the teaching sequence found in the classrooms studied is a teacher's question, a pupil's response, and more often than not, a teacher's reaction to that response'. In this study 72 per cent of classroom talk was shown to be by the teacher, and of this slightly less than 7 per cent was devoted to responding to pupil-initiated talk, the rest consisting of asking questions, focusing pupils' attention on topics and commenting on what they say.

The kinds of questions the teacher asks will reveal to the pupil the kind of thinking which is expected of him.

Stevens (1912) found that the teachers he studied asked 66 per cent memory-type questions drawn directly from the textbook. What is more startling is that in a study conducted fifty years later, Floyd (1966) determined that over 75 per cent of the teachers' questions in his sample required specific fact answers.

Taba, Levine and Elzey (1964) and Hunkins (1972) have shown that different types of questions stimulate different kinds of thinking, therefore it is important for the teacher to be conscious of the purpose of his questions.

Classifying questions

There are many ways of classifying questions, and most of these classifications are useful in that they provide a conceptual framework for looking at them. One of the best-known classifications is Bloom's *Taxonomy of Educational Objectives* (1956). There are six levels of Bloom's *Taxonomy*, and questions at each level require a response which uses a different kind of thought process.

You should be able to formulate questions on each of these six levels in order to encourage your pupils to employ a variety of cognitive processes. The six levels are:
1. Knowledge.
2. Comprehension.
3. Application.
4. Analysis.
5. Synthesis.
6. Evaluation.

Knowledge

When your purpose is to determine whether pupils remember certain specific facts, ask recall questions.

Examples: (a) When did Henry VIII become King of England?
(b) Name two kinds of blood-vessels in the body.
(c) Who wrote the play *A Midsummer's Night Dream*?
(d) What is the capital of France?

Recall is observable when a pupil states specific facts or gives information in much the same form as it was previously presented by the teacher or in textual material. A recall answer does not go beyond the information previously presented, nor does it change the form or organization of the information. Answers can be easily judged as right or wrong if compared with the original source. Also included will be information which is acquired through everyday experience. For example: 'What do we buy from the post office?' This knowledge category is critical to other levels of thinking. We cannot ask pupils to think at higher levels if they lack fundamental information.

Although important, this category has some drawbacks. The main one is that teachers tend to over-use it. Another drawback is that knowledge questions assess only a superficial understanding, and lastly much of what is memorized is rapidly forgotten.

Words often found in knowledge questions are:

Who?	define
What?	recall
Where?	recognize
When?	name

Although the most frequent type of recall questions call for brief responses, not all recall questions call for brief answers.

For example: 'Give the names of the thirty heaviest elements and their atomic weights' requires the recall of a set of related facts; or 'What was Darwin's theory of evolution' requires the recall of an entire theory.

Comprehension

When your purpose is to help pupils organize facts in such a way as to make some sense of them, ask comprehension questions. These questions will require the pupil to select those facts that are pertinent in order to describe, compare or contrast.

Examples: (a) Describe the kinds of problems faced by immigrants.

(b) Compare the duties of the House of Commons with those of the House of Lords.

(c) How did life in the eighteenth century differ from life today?

Sometimes comprehension questions also require pupils to translate ideas from one medium to another, for instance to interpret material presented in the form of graphs or tables.

Examples: (d) From the above graph give the average annual rainfall for this country.

(e) Using the table of plant counts made in the years 1965–70, name the dominant species in 1968.

It is important to remember that the information necessary to answer comprehension questions should already have been provided for the pupil.

Words commonly found in comprehension questions are:

Describe	put in your own words
Compare	
	explain
Contrast	

Application

When your purpose is to encourage your pupils to apply information they have learned in order to reach an answer to a problem, ask application questions. These questions require the pupils to apply a rule or process to a problem in order to determine the correct answer.

Examples: (a) In mathematics, for instance, application questions are very common:
If $x = 2$ and $y = 5$
Then $x^2 + 2y = \qquad$?

But application questions are also used in other subject areas:

(b) In geography when a pupil is asked to locate a point on a map by applying the definitions he has already learned of latitude and longitude.

(c) In biology when a pupil is asked to apply what he has learned about populations by answering the question: 'When organisms are living densely packed in a small area are they more likely to compete if they belong to one species than if they belong to many different species?'

(d) In English language when a pupil is asked, 'Give three examples of adjectives', in order to apply the definition he has been given.

Words commonly found or implicit in application questions are:

Apply	employ
Classify	give an example
Use	
Choose	

Analysis

When your purpose is to help pupils not only to remember and organize information, but also to analyse it for underlying reasons such as cause and effect, explanatory-type questions are asked.

1. To identify motives, reasons and causes for a specific occurrence.

Examples: 'What factors influenced Britain's decision to join the EEC?'
'Why was scurvy once a common disease among sailors?'

2. To consider and analyse available information in order to reach a conclusion.
    Examples: 'After reading the *Forsyte Saga*, what is your impression of the author's view of society of his time?'
    'Now that your experiments are complete, what is your conclusion about the factors affecting the growth of seedlings?'

3. To analyse a conclusion, inference or generalization based on evidence.
    Examples: 'What causes children to disagree with their parents?'
    'In what ways have public health measures contributed to a worsening of the state of the human population?'

Analysis questions require critical thinking from pupils. A pupil is unable to answer an analysis question by repeating information. Analysis questions require pupils to analyse information in order to identify causes, to reach conclusions or to find evidence.

Words frequently used in analysis questions are:

Why?
What factors?
Draw conclusions
Determine evidence (support, analyse)

Synthesis

When your purpose is to help pupils to form relationships and put things together in new or original ways, ask synthesis questions. These questions are used to help develop the creative abilities of pupils. Such questions test a thorough understanding of a subject and may require pupils to make predictions, to make original communications or to solve problems. Although application questions also require pupils to solve problems, synthesis questions differ from these in that they do not require answers to problems that have a single correct answer, but instead, allow a variety of creative answers.

Examples: 'What do you suppose would happen if we ran out of coal and oil?'

'Under what conditions might countries of the world be likely to unite?'

'How would you summarize the effect of the socialist movement in improving the conditions of working people?'

Words and phrases often found in synthesis questions are:
> Predict
> Produce
> Write
> Develop
> What would happen if ...?

Evaluation

When your purpose is to help pupils choose among alternatives by judging which best fits some stated value, ask evaluation questions. These questions do not have a single correct answer but require the pupil to judge the merit of an idea, a solution to a problem or an aesthetic work. They may also ask the pupil to offer an opinion.

Examples: 'Which story most accurately describes life on an English farm?'

'Should this statement be defended or rejected? For what reasons?'

'Which topic shall we select for study next? How would you justify this choice?'

'Do you consider that a factory which pollutes a river should be closed, even if this will result in unemployment?'

'How much do you think our present society would be willing to restrict the convenience of personal travel by car to save energy?'

Words often used in evaluation questions are:
> Judge
> Assess
> Decide
> Justify

Teachers' questions and pupils' responses

Remember that all teachers' questions are categorized on the basis of the anticipated pupil's answer. All pupils' answers, however, are categorized only on the basis of the kind and level of thinking revealed by the actual verbal response.

Most frequently teachers' questions and pupils' answers will be consistent, but that is not always the case. Although a teacher may ask for manipulation of information or explanation of a preference, a pupil may not do so. Again a teacher may ask only for recall and a pupil may go beyond the question in his answer. This is illustrated in the following example:

Teacher: In what areas of Britain can one see the effects of glaciation? (Lower order: asks for recall)

Pupil 1: The Highlands of Scotland. (Lower order: remembers information)

Pupil 2: Usually in mountainous areas where the ice has smoothed off the mountain tops and there are moraines left by melting glaciers. (Higher order: relates the effect of ice to land forms)

Teacher: Can you compare the effects of a glacier and a river on land formation? (Higher order: asks pupil to make a comparison)

Pupil 1: A glacier produces a U-shaped valley and a river a V-shaped valley. (Lower order: recall of information)

Pupil 2: A river and a glacier both erode the land, but a glacier would be more forceful and would produce a valley of a different shape from that produced by a river. (Higher order: both a comparison and a judgement is made and reasons for it given)

Summary

In order to categorize a teacher's question one must determine the kind of thinking required on the part of the pupil in order to answer this question. Questions can be subdivided according to the level of cognitive thought required. Lower-order questions require the pupil to recall information. Higher-order questions require the pupil to manipulate information for some purpose.

Summary chart of lower-order and higher-order thinking

Characteristics of lower-order thinking

Remembers specific ...	Facts or Information which were Previously Taught or are General Knowledge

Characteristics of higher-order thinking

Changes the form of information in order to ...	Compare or Contrast or Explain or Summarize or Analyse or Synthesize or Evaluate

Lower-order questions

Recall is observable when a pupil states specific facts or information in much the same form as it was previously presented by the teacher or in textual material.

A recall answer does not go beyond the information previously presented nor does it change the form or organization of the information. Answers can easily be judged as right or wrong compared with the original source. Also included would be information which is generally acquired through everyday experience, e.g. 'What do we buy from the post office?'

Higher-order questions

Higher-order thinking is observable when a pupil changes the form or organization of information in order to compare, contrast, summarize, extend, apply, analyse, reorganize or evaluate its content to resolve a problem.

In order to answer a higher-order question a pupil may recall or be given information, but he must go beyond that and manipulate or use the information to produce an answer which differs in form and organization from the form in which it was previously encountered. Higher-order answers may be judged by such standards as logic, rationality and objectivity on scales from good to bad, but are less susceptible to single judgements of right or wrong.

Summary chart of question categories

Question category and some key words or phrases	Level of thinking required from the pupil	Examples
Recall Who? What? Where? When? Define.	Recall of facts, observations or definitions.	1. What is the capital of France? 2. When did Columbus discover America?
Comprehension Describe, Compare, Contrast, Explain, Rephrase.	Giving descriptions. Stating main ideas. Comparing and contrasting.	1. Explain in your own words the problems faced by immigrants. 2. Compare the duties of the House of Commons with those of the House of Lords.
Application Apply, Solve, Classify, Select, Employ, Use.	Applying rules and techniques to solve problems having a single correct answer.	1. What is the latitude of London? 2. Classify these animals. 3. If you were planning to sunbathe, what time of the day are you most likely to become sunburned?
Analysis Why? Identify cause or reason. Conclude, Infer, Deduce, Determine the evidence. Draw a conclusion.	Identifying motives or causes. Making inferences. Finding evidence to support generalizations.	1. *Why* do you think Britain hesitated to join the European Economic Community? 2. What does this book tell us about the author's attitude to society?

		3. What evidence can you find to support Darwin's theory of natural selection?
Synthesis Solve (more than one correct answer). Predict, Propose, Plan, Write, Develop.	Solving problems. Making predictions. Producing original communications.	1. What actions could the government take to control population growth? 2. What do you predict would happen if we ran out of coal and oil? 3. Write a story based on life in the eighteenth century.
Evaluation Judge, Evaluate, Decide, Appraise. What in your opinion?	Giving opinions on issues. Judging the validity of ideas. Judging the merit of the solution to a problem. Judging the merit of art and literature.	1. Which topic shall we select for study next? How do you justify this choice? 2. Do you think it is true that newspapers influence public opinion? 3. Should this statement be defended or rejected? Give your reasons. 4. Some people think the government should take action to control population growth in India. Do you agree? 5. What in your opinion is abstract art?

Exercise 4.1

Use the space before each question to categorize the question as
L (lower order) or H (higher order).
Check your answers with the answer key given below.

1. _____ Who discovered America?
2. _____ What characteristics do all mammals share?
3. _____ What is the difference between an acid and a base?
4. _____ Use your atlas to find the latitude of Paris.
5. _____ What is the meaning of 'effervescent'?
6. _____ Why have the leaves on this plant shrivelled?
7. _____ If attendance at school was not compulsory what would happen?
8. _____ Who discovered radium?
9. _____ How can we find out if this is a diamond?
10. _____ Do you think it is true that over-population will lead to mass starvation?

Answer key: 1 L, 2 H, 3 H, 4 H, 5 L, 6 H, 7 H, 8 L, 9 H, 10 H.

Exercise 4.2

Read the following passage:

Increase in births goes on
United Nations (NY) 30 Jan. 1977.

The world's population totalled 3967 millions in mid 1975, showing a one-year increase of 77 millions, the latest edition of the UN Demographic Yearbook reported today. If this annual growth rate is maintained, the global population will double in 37 years.

According to the latest figures, more than half the world's people – 2256 millions or some 56.9 per cent – live in Asia. Some 473 millions, or 11.9 per cent live in Europe, 401 millions (10.1%) in Africa, 324 millions (8.2%) in Latin America, 255 millions (6.4%) in the Soviet Union, 237 millions (6%) in North America and 21.3 millions (0.3%) in Oceania.

The most rapid population growth is taking place in Africa where the annual rate is 2 per cent or more, in 40 of the 47 countries or areas for which figures are available. 10 of them have rates of 3 per cent or above. In Europe, 26 out of the 37 countries reported an annual increase of less than 1 per cent.

Baby girls in Norway enjoy the world's longest life expectancy – 77.6 years. Figures for most African nations show a life expectancy of less than 50 years. In 19 it is less than 40 years.

(Reuter, *The Guardian*, 1977.)

Classify these questions using the following key: R for recall, C for comprehension, Ap. for application, An. for analysis, S for synthesis and E for evaluation.

1. Which population enjoys the world's longest life expectancy according to the survey reported here? _____
2. Why is the most rapid population growth taking place in Africa? _____
3. What factors will be likely to reduce the rapid population growth taking place in Africa? _____
4. What is the percentage increase in population for the whole world? _____
5. What does this passage tell us about the distribution of the world's population? _____
6. What is the meaning of 'demographic'? _____
7. Why has Europe the lowest population growth rate? _____
8. What problems are likely to occur in those countries with rapidly growing populations? _____
9. In some countries the government takes specific measures to control population growth. Do you agree with this approach? _____
10. Assuming that we wish to control the population, what actions can private citizens take to control population growth? _____

Answer key: 1 R, 2 An., 3 S, 4 Ap., 5 C, 6 R, 7 An., 8 S, 9 E, 10 S.

Exercise 4.3

Read the following passage:

Tokyo: a city struggling to breathe

In the summer of this year Tokyo's long-suffering citizens experienced their first taste of a new and most unpleasant hazard: Photochemical smog. This phenomenon, known also in Los Angeles, occurs when unburnt hydrocarbons and nitrogen oxides contained in car exhaust fumes are subjected to strong sunlight. It is invisible – or very nearly – but deadly.

The Tokyo version, sharpened by noxious sulphur gases borne on southerly summer winds from the coastal industrial zones of Kawasaki and Yokohama, proved particularly vicious. The winds were seldom strong enough to clear the still, humid air of the capital itself.

The first evidence of the disagreeable properties of the new hazard was a report that a group of children playing in a schoolyard had found trouble breathing and begun falling down. In the days and weeks that followed thousands of people had to be treated in Tokyo hospitals for painfully smarting eyes and sore throats.

A system of smog warnings was quickly established: on bad days radio and television announcers, and touring loudspeaker vans, exhorted residents to stay indoors and motorists to leave their cars at home. Children were advised not to play in the open air. It was all rather reminiscent, as some older Japanese remarked, of the air raid warnings of World War Two.

Pollution is now just another aspect of living in Tokyo. Mr Michitaka Kaino the director of the Pollution Research Centre, foresees the day when the pedestrian will carry a gas mask as naturally as an umbrella. He has predicted that air pollution will increase 500 times in the next 10 years.

A Tokyo department store has been doing a brisk trade since August in small, portable oxygen generators. They sell at about £15.

Many of Tokyo's justly famous cedars and pines are dying in the city's polluted air. Even the well tended flora in the grounds of the imperial palace are not immune. Animals and birds that have died at Tokyo zoo have been found to have completely blackened lungs.

The effects on human health have been under study since 1966. Many cases of bronchial asthma, chronic bronchitis, pulmonary emphysema and other respiratory diseases are thought to be closely related to air pollution.

Air pollution has posed a problem in Tokyo since about 1960 when cheap, sulphur-laden Middle East oil replaced coal as the main fuel. Factories burn oil all the year round, office buildings and private homes use it in winter for heating. Together they pump some 1.7 million tons of noxious gases, mainly sulphur dioxide, into the atmosphere every year.

To this must be added the exhaust fumes of the two million or so cars clogging Tokyo's streets. The whole unpleasant mess is frequently compounded by a combination of atmospheric factors that prevent the pollutants in the air from rising and dispersing in the normal way.

The government has only very belatedly begun to take any action. Early last year limits were set on the discharge of sulphur dioxide by factories. But industry is being allowed a leisurely ten years to conform to the new standards. Office buildings are not affected at all (though this winter measures may be taken against them for the first time).

In February this year, the government approved a recommendation by the transport ministry that the carbon monoxide content of car exhaust fumes should be kept to 4.5 per cent in new cars and 5.5 per cent in old cars. However, little or no pressure has been brought on the car manufacturers themselves to help reduce pollution. Significantly, only export car models are fitted with exhaust emission controls.

(From The Times, 25 November 1970)

Now prepare questions you might ask your class on the material in the above passage. Prepare questions in each of the categories listed below:
1. Recall.
2. Comprehension.
3. Application.
4. Analysis.
5. Synthesis.
6. Evaluation.

You may wish to compare your questions with some examples given below:

Recall

What are the causes of photochemical smog?

Comprehension

Describe how you can tell if the air is polluted.

Application

Select one control which could be easily applied to improve air pollution in Tokyo.

Analysis

Why is the air allowed to become polluted?

Synthesis

What could be done to control photochemical smog?

Evaluation

Do you think that the newspaper was justified in using this headline?

Additional reading

Hunkins, F. P. (1972) *Questioning Strategies and Techniques*, Allyn and Bacon, Boston.
Sanders, N. M. (1966) *Classroom Questions: What Kinds?* Harper and Row, London.
Bloom, B. S. ed. (1956) *Taxonomy of Educational Objectives*, Longman, London.

Chapter 5

Using questions in classroom discussion

The last chapter has demonstrated that the kinds of questions the teacher asks reveal to the pupil the kind of thinking which is expected of him. Research studies carried out in many parts of the world have shown that the majority of teachers' questions call for specific fact answers, or lower cognitive thought. But we have seen that higher cognitive questions, which cause pupils to go beyond memory and use other thought processes in forming an answer have an important role. While both types of questions have their part to play in teaching, a heavy reliance on lower-order questioning encourages rote learning and does little to develop higher-order thinking processes.

In a study made on samples of in-service teachers in the USA, Borg et al. (1970) showed that only 38 per cent of the questions used in discussion were in the higher-order category, before training, but that after fifteen hours of training, involving the study and practice of questioning skills, the percentage of questions in the higher-order category was significantly increased (50%). A similar study made on samples of experienced English teachers in 1975 (Perrott et al. 1975a) showed that 47 per cent of their discussion questions were in the higher-order category before training and that after fifteen hours of training involving the study and practice of questioning skills, both the percentage of higher-order questions asked by teachers and the percentage of higher-order responses given by their pupils showed a significant increase. The percentage of higher-order questions increased from 47 to 64, while the percentage of higher-order responses increased from 50 to 67.

The questioning skills in which teachers received training in the studies quoted above are shown in Table 5.1

The primary objective of using all the skills listed below is to

Table 5.1 Using questions to improve the quality and quantity of pupils' participation in discussion

Objectives	Related teaching skills
A. To help pupils to give more complete and thoughtful responses	1. Pausing 2. Prompting 3. Seeking further clarification 4. Refocusing a pupil's response
B. To increase the amount and quality of pupils' participation	1. Redirecting the same question to several pupils 2. Framing questions that call for sets of related facts 3. Framing questions that require the pupil to use higher cognitive thought

improve the quality and quantity of pupils' participation. The related teaching skills require action on the part of the teacher to enable this improvement to come about. For instance, teachers in Borg's American samples (1970) talked for 53 per cent of the discussion time, while teachers in Perrott et al's (1975a) English samples talked for 75 per cent of the time before training. After training in the teaching skills listed above, the amount of teacher talk in the American sample was reduced to 33 per cent of the discussion time and in the English samples to 53 per cent of the time (OECD Report, 1975), allowing for the corresponding increase in pupils' participation. In other words, teaching skills are a means to an end (pupils' behaviour) not an end in themselves (teacher behaviour). Therefore, you must have clearly in mind the particular end you wish to achieve and carefully observe pupils' behaviour in order to determine when a particular skill is appropriate. In effect, you must become a careful observer of pupils' behaviour, since their reactions can give you valuable clues about the effectiveness of your own performance.

Helping pupils to give more complete and thoughtful responses

Pausing

Before we discuss pausing, let us look at the common practice of 'rapid-fire questioning', or calling on a pupil to respond immediately after a question. If the teacher's objective is to sample what the class knows within a relatively short time and to elicit brief answers, 'rapid-fire questioning' is an appropriate skill.

On the other hand, if the teacher's objective is to provide an atmosphere more conducive to discussion, in which pupils will have time to organize longer and more thoughtful responses, he must adopt a more appropriate questioning procedure. One skill that may be used to encourage longer and more thoughtful responses is to pause for three to five seconds after asking a question, but before calling on a pupil. The use of this skill should eventually result in longer responses because your pupils will be able to discriminate between pausing behaviour and your 'rapid-fire questioning'.

The very long pause used to promote recall or rote memory is a different skill from that with which we are concerned here. Whereas teachers may use a long pause of the 'come on, you should all have your hands up' variety, the objective differs in that it is intended to provide time for the organization of longer, more thoughtful responses. You can help your pupils make this distinction by telling them why you are pausing and reminding them when you do not obtain satisfactory responses.

Pausing eventually serves a twofold function in your classroom:
1. It provides an atmosphere more conducive to discussion than 'rapid-fire questioning' produces.
2. The pupils learn to use the pause to organize a more complete answer.

However, they will not automatically give longer answers when you first begin using pausing in your discussions. Depending upon their previous classroom experiences, relatively few pupils may respond appropriately. Some may begin to day-dream, hoping they will not be called on; others may raise their hands without first thinking. Therefore, when you first start using pausing behaviour, you should help the pupils learn what you want them to do. Immediately after the question verbal prompts can be presented, such as, 'Please think over your answer carefully', 'When I call on you, I want a complete answer', then pause for three to five seconds before you call on someone.

By giving these verbal prompts when you begin to use pausing systematically, you help to establish your pausing behaviour as a signal that you want longer responses. A given behaviour on your part becomes meaningful to the pupil only when you show what is expected of him. The verbal prompting can be gradually dropped, and eventually your pause will be all that is necessary to obtain more complex responses from your pupils.

This process illustrates that behaviour, even complex social interactions, can be analysed and controlled. For instance, when you pause after a question, your behaviour is a signal to the pupil that you want some specific kind of response. In turn, if he gives a more complex answer, you praise him, thus reinforcing his appropriate behaviour.

However, since most teachers ask far too many questions requiring short answers (Floyd 1960) many pupils have acquired the habit of responding as briefly as possible to almost any question. If you want to help pupils give longer, more thoughtful responses you must also examine the type of question you are using. You may be using types of questions associated with short answers. One such type is the yes/no question, e.g. 'Isn't the purpose of our local police force the protection of life and property?'

Another variant is a little more subtle. In this instance the teacher appears to be calling for a longer response, but the question is so phrased that a brief answer will suffice, e.g. 'Would you say that the Crusades were a failure?' The same question could be asked in another way, 'What reasons could you give for saying either that the Crusades were a success or that they were a failure?' This question is so phrased that a 'yes' or 'no' response will not suffice here (Groisser 1964).

Success lies in using questions which require longer and more thoughtful responses, pausing to allow ample time to organize those responses and reinforcing pupils for such responses.

When the pupil responds to a question, you should have a clear idea of the kind of response you want. By this is meant that you should have some idea of the concepts which are likely to be included in an acceptable answer. In order to accomplish this during questioning you should always prepare criterion responses along with your questions before class. This criterion response should contain those ideas which you think are necessary for an acceptable answer or other standards which will be used to determine acceptability.

Some examples of such standards are given below:

1. Content – includes certain essential facts or ideas.
2. Clarity – speaks clearly and finishes ideas.

3. Appropriateness – answers the question that was asked.
4. Support – gives reasons and examples to support the answer.
5. Complexity – tells how he arrived at the answer and why.
6. Originality – uses imagination to answer in an unusual way.

Whatever criteria you use, if the pupil's response does not come up to the level you are seeking, you must be prepared to help him to develop a better answer. Good ideas, however, should not be rejected simply because you did not previously consider them. You should always be prepared to evaluate and accept good answers, and to reinforce the pupil for them.

To bring the pupil's response up to a higher level, you must listen carefully to what he says. If you pause, and then accept a 'yes' or 'no' answer, pausing will not mean anything special since any kind of answer will appear to be acceptable. Pausing becomes meaningful to the pupil only if you react to the response in such a manner as to indicate that pausing is your signal for a more complete and thoughtful answer.

Here are examples of correct and incorrect teacher responses:

Correct (Teacher): What evidence do you see around you of air pollution?

(Pause)

(Pupil): It's smoggy.

(Teacher): Would you enlarge on that?

Incorrect (Teacher): What evidence do you see around you of air pollution?

(Pause)

(Pupil): It's smoggy.

(Teacher): Good.

Note that in the first instance the teacher did not accept an incomplete response. The pupil is being required to extend his answer to meet the criterion of a more complete response. The teacher in the second example accepted an inadequate answer after pausing. As a result the pupil is likely to continue giving partial or less complex responses.

Exercise 5.1

Prepare a microlesson lasting ten minutes in which you practise, pausing three to five seconds after asking a question.

In planning the lesson try to formulate questions which are appropriate to the use of this skill, i.e. note when it is appropriate to require a long and complex response as one of the criteria for an acceptable answer.

Use the lesson plan form given below to help in preparing your microlesson.

Lesson plan form

Objective: To use pausing after asking a question to elicit longer and more complete answers.

Lesson topic: _____

_____

Planned questions	**Criteria**
1. _____	_____
_____	_____
_____	_____
2. _____	_____
_____	_____
_____	_____
3. _____	_____
_____	_____

Notes: _____

_____

_____

Arrange to audio-record your lesson.

Evaluation (Exercise 5.1)

Purpose: To evaluate your use of questioning and pausing to elicit more complex and longer responses.

Procedure for recording observations

Select a five-minute sample of your recording for this evaluation. After each instance of pausing make a tally on the evaluation form given below. If necessary stop the tape at these points.

You may use a stop-watch or a watch with a sweep-second hand to estimate pausing time after each question. A question is defined as an uninterrupted query directed toward a single pupil. Indicate by a tick whether, after each question, there was no pause, a pause of less than three seconds, or a pause of three seconds or more.

After each pupil response tick the box which describes the length of the response. Indicate whether you reinforced the pupil's response, by ticking 'yes' or 'no'.

Appraisal guide: Pausing

Questions		1	2	3	4	5	6	7	8	9	10	TOTAL
Pause	No pause											
	Pause less than 3 sec											
	Pause 3 sec or more											
Response	One word											
	10 words or less											
	More than 10 words											
Reinforcement	Yes											
	No											

Comments

Interpretation

Pausing allows pupils to organize more complex and longer responses. If you are not receiving longer, more complex answers, analyse your tallies for the following possible explanations:

1. A large proportion of minimal (or no) pauses, leaving insufficient time to form complex responses.
2. Using negative reinforcement or rewarding unacceptable responses, thus preventing recognition that more complex responses are desired.
3. Asking questions which do not require complex or longer responses.

In the previous exercise you practised the problem of eliciting more complex and longer responses from pupils. If the initial response is inadequate, the teacher then faces the problem of modifying the response to match some predetermined criterion. Let us assume that this initially weak response can be classified somewhere on a continuum from 'I don't know' to what the teacher thinks is an acceptable (criterion) response.

The next three skills presented in this section are intended to develop the initial response. They are: Prompting; Seeking Clarification; Refocusing. The specific skill used depends on the location of the initial answer on the continuum. The general name given to these skills is probing. Probing involves a series of questions addressed to one pupil and is designed to develop his initial response into a more adequate answer.

Prompting

Prompting is the probing skill used when the pupil gives:
(a) an 'I don't know' response;
(b) a very weak response;
(c) a partly or completely incorrect response.

Let us begin with the situation in which a pupil fails to respond, or gives an 'I don't know' response. After such a response, you might well rephrase the question in order to examine the possibility that the question was either ambiguous or too vague.

For example, the question, 'What do you think about war?' is undoubtedly much more ambiguous than the same question phrased, 'Why has war been called a necessary evil?' Similarly, you are likely to receive a better response from 'What are some of the factors that influence the growth of our teeth?' than from 'How do teeth grow?' In fact, a precise question often contains prompts to help the pupil organize his response (Groisser 1964).

If your question seems clear enough, begin prompting. Prompting strategy is based on a series of questions containing hints that help the pupil develop his answer. Frequently you can begin by referring to material that he does know. For example, a pupil may not be able to answer a question about the effects of the Black Death, but he may begin to respond to a series of questions beginning with 'What happened during the Black Death?', followed by 'Why could plague spread easily and quickly throughout the land in the fourteenth century?' Conceivably, you might have to return to an even simpler level until you find some related material from which you can begin the prompting sequence. Often the questions may contain direct hints, for example, 'What happens when we have a 'flu epidemic in our country?'

Sometimes a single prompt will be sufficient to guide the pupil to a better answer. More commonly, it is necessary for the teacher to use a series of prompts which lead the pupil step by step to answer the original question. Teacher prompts may be in the form of intermediate questions, clues or hints, that give the pupil the information he needs to arrive at a better answer. The essential characteristics of prompting are as follows:

1. The teacher asks a question.
2. The pupil gives an 'I don't know' or weak reply.
3. The teacher gives the same pupil a hint or asks a question designed to lead him to a better answer to the initial question.
4. The teacher may use a single prompt or a series of prompts to guide the pupil to a better answer to the initial question.
5. The prompts are directed to the same pupil who was asked the initial question, or to the pupil who responded last if the question has been redirected.

If the initial response is partly correct, first reinforce the correct part by telling the pupil what was right. Then begin by modifying the incorrect part. The exact questions used in a prompting sequence cannot be specified in advance, since each depends on the pupil's previous response. However, you should always have in mind the criterion response. Equally important, you should praise the final answer as much as if the pupil gave it at the beginning.

Seeking clarification

In some instances a pupil may give a response which is poorly organized, lacking in detail or incomplete. Here you face a situation in which the pupil is not wrong, but in which his answer still does not match the response you seek. Under these circumstances you can use the probing skill of seeking clarification. Unlike prompting, seeking clarification starts at a different point on the response continuum. The teacher is not adding information; he is requesting the pupil to do so. Examples of probes for further clarification include:

'How can you make your answer clearer?'

'Can you state that another way?'

All these call for additional information. Note that these questions do not include any of the hints or clues that are characteristic of prompting.

Clarification may also be used when the pupil gives an answer that is basically satisfactory, but which the teacher believes can be improved by the pupil if he will elaborate or discuss his answer further. In this case the teacher may ask the pupil why he gave the answer, or ask him to justify or explain his response. Generally, only one request for clarification is given. However, occasionally the pupil's subsequent responses will still require clarification and further requests will be made by the teacher.

Examples of clarification questions that may be used to encourage a pupil to justify his answer include:

'Can you restate your answer? I am not quite sure I understand you completely?'

'Can you tell me why you think you are right?'

When a pupil is asked to justify his response, you should monitor closely the underlying rationale and help to clarify any faulty assumptions.

Refocusing

There are numerous occasions when the teacher receives a response that matches the one he wants. Refocusing may then be used to relate the pupil's response to another topic he has studied.

The skill is used to help the pupil consider the implications of his response within a broader conceptual framework. He is asked to relate his answer to another issue.

Example A. Idea: Rules and laws are intended to govern behaviour.

Teacher: How do the players know what they are and are not allowed to do while they are playing soccer?

James: There are rules and if you break the rules a penalty is given.

Teacher: How does this relate to our studies of government?

(Refocus)

James: I suppose laws are like rules. If you break the law in some way, you are punished.

Example B. Idea: People's beliefs influence their behaviour.

Teacher: The Watusi believed their cows were sacred. Andrew, how did this belief influence their behaviour?

Andrew: Even when there was a famine they would not eat their cows. They would starve.

Teacher: How was this case similar to what we read about the Sepoy rebellion, Andrew?

(Refocus)

Andrew: The Sepoys were soldiers in the British Army in India. Someone told them that the cartridges used in their guns were greased with fat from pigs. Before a soldier loaded the guns he had to bite the cartridge. Because the Sepoys were Muslims they believed this was against their religion and rebelled.

Refocusing is a probing skill that is used at the highest level in the continuun that we discussed earlier. It is the most difficult form of probing since the teacher must have a thorough knowledge of how various topics in the curriculum may be related. You will be able to refocus more effectively if you study the content of your planned discussion beforehand, and note relationships with other topics the class has studied.

Probing skills compared
In attempting to discriminate between prompting and seeking further clarification, keep in mind the following points.

Prompting is generally used when the pupil gives an 'I don't know' or very weak answer. Further clarification is generally used with initial pupil answers of better quality. These answers are minimally acceptable, but can be improved by asking the pupil to clarify or elaborate his answer.

In prompting, the teacher either gives hints or asks leading questions regarding the topic of the initial question. In seeking further clarification, the teacher asks the pupil to add to his answer by clarifying, justifying his point of view or explaining. Seeking further clarification does not involve the use of hints or the use of leading questions.

In either case the teacher's strategy is to lead the pupil back to answering the original question.

In some instances the teacher asks a question and the pupil's response is essentially satisfactory, but the teacher wishes to relate this response to another topic that the class has studied. The teacher's request to refocus the response on another topic is often started with phrases such as 'How does this relate to ...?' The refocusing question must come from a pupil's response. However, unlike prompting or seeking further clarification, the question may be directed to the whole class and a different pupil called on to answer.

Obviously, it is possible for a teacher to use more than one probing skill in a probing sequence. Since the teacher's probing behaviour is dependent on the pupil's response, a teacher may question, prompt, seek clarification and refocus, all in the same sequence. However, a series of questions on the same topic does not necessarily constitute probing simply because they are related to the same topic or directed to the same pupil.

Example: Teacher: Do you enjoy being a boy scout, John?
Pupil: Yes.
Teacher: How old were you when you joined?
Pupil: Twelve.
Teacher: How many times a week do you go to a meeting?
Pupil: Twice a week.
Teacher: Are many of your friends in the scouts?
Pupil: Yes.

These questions are separate and discrete. The teacher is not leading the pupil towards a specific answer, asking for clarification of a particular answer, or requesting that a pupil relate this to some other topic. The teacher is merely asking a series of questions related to the same topic.

Failure to probe

In order to help pupils arrive at better answers, a teacher must have a clear idea of what constitutes a good answer, and must be able to rate each pupil's response in terms of that good answer. Frequently teachers with poor probing skills tend to redirect incorrect or unsatisfactory answers under the guise of one pupil helping another.

Example 1:   Teacher: Tell me something about the way of life of the pygmies in the Congo.
            Pupil: I don't know.
            Teacher: Can you help him, John?

Example 2:   Teacher: Why is the west side of Britain warmer than the east side in winter?
            Pupil: I think it's something to do with the sea.
            Teacher: Exactly what do you mean?
            Pupil: (Silence)
            Teacher: Can someone else explain?

In the first example the teacher fails to probe. In the second example, the teacher attempts to probe but discontinues before an acceptable answer is given. Since the number of probes required to reach a satisfactory answer is determined by the pupil's responses, a probing sequence may require one prompt or a series of probes. The frequent occurrence of long probing sequences, however, is rare, primarily because the teacher feels that other pupils are neglected when they concentrate on the thinking of one pupil. Possibly because of this, teachers tend to err in the direction of insufficient probing of a pupil's responses. As a teacher becomes more skilled in the use of probing, longer sequences will require less time and increase the teacher's effectiveness in helping pupils develop acceptable responses.

Probing skills can produce a teacher–pupil dialogue that results in a better understanding of the lesson materials. An equally important advantage is that probing skills enable the teacher to modify a pupil's responses in a positive manner without resorting to the negative reinforcement of aversive value statements.

Exercise 5.2

In the example below, notice how the teacher uses probing skills within

the context of an extended discussion. In the appropriate space, identify the numbered examples of probing using the following key:
P Prompting; C Clarification; R Refocusing.

Teacher: We have been talking about the characteristics of really great men and we seem to be having difficulty in deciding what the really important characteristics are. What do you think Sandra?

Sandra: I think a really great man is one who does something important for a lot of people.

1. _____ Teacher: Could you explain your idea further?

Sandra: Well, some people are famous or important because of who they are or what they do, but I don't think this makes them great unless their life has made things better or happier for other people. That's what being great means.

Teacher: Brian, do you agree with Sandra?

Brian: Being great seems to mean being famous. I think I agree that if you do anything people remember, it makes you famous and so you must be great.

Teacher: Does this mean that anyone who is famous is 'great', Jane?

Jane: I don't know.

2. _____ Teacher: Do you think Hitler was great?

Jane: No, I don't.

3. _____ Teacher: Do you think he was famous?

Jane: Yes, everyone remembers him. But he wasn't a good man.

4. _____ Teacher: Does that make any difference?

Jane: I suppose a man has to be good to be great. Being famous or remembered is not enough. You can be remembered for being bad and that doesn't make you great. I suppose a man is only great if he is remembered for doing something good like helping his country or painting beautiful pictures.

Teacher: Does everyone agree with Jane, that a really great man is one who is remembered for doing something good?

Edward: I don't think it matters.

5. _____ Teacher: What do you mean, Edward?

Edward: Whether you're remembered or famous. I think a lot of people we never hear about are great because of the way they live. Like people who suffer and don't complain, or people who do what they believe is right even when it's hard.

6. _____ Teacher: Can you relate that idea to something we all know about?

   Edward: I can't think.

7. _____ Teacher: What about the Second World War?

   Edward: Yes, a lot of people went about their lives and kept up their spirits even when they were being bombed. People who did that were great even if no one knows who they were.

   Michael: But it's got to be unusual too. Not everyone who leads a good life or does something good is great.

8. _____ Teacher: Can you add anything further to that Michael?

   Michael: I agree that a great man is good or does good and I agree that no one has to know about it, but it has to be unusual. He has to be different from most men. Better I suppose, a lot better.

Answer key: 1 C, 2 P, 3 P, 4 P, 5 C, 6 R, 7 P, 8 C.

Exercise 5.3

Circle the correct answer.

1. A pupil answers 'I don't know' to your original question. What should you do next?
   a. Redirect the original question to another pupil.
   b. Rephrase the original question.
   c. Formulate a prompting question which is simpler than the first.

2. A pupil has given a complete answer to your question but you suspect that he may be guessing in part. Which of the following would be the most appropriate response?
   a. Can you elaborate on your answer?
   b. I think you guessed.
   c. Can anyone else add anything?

3. Probing a pupil about the issues involved in the 'generation gap', the teacher has asked him, 'What do you and your parents argue about?' The skill the teacher used is:
   a. Rephrasing the question.
   b. Prompting by using personal experience.
   c. Asking for further clarification.

4. A pupil fails to answer the question: 'Why do the astronauts weigh less on the moon than on earth?' Which of the following would be a good starting prompt to lead the pupil towards the idea of gravity?
   a. Not only do the astronauts weigh less, they can jump higher. Why?

    b. How much less do the astronauts weigh on the moon?

    c. How much do you weigh yourself?

5. Consider this pupil-teacher exchange:

    Teacher: How might we decide whether television accurately presents the news?

    Pupil: I don't know.

    Teacher: Well, in what other ways do we get the news?

    Pupil: By listening to the radio and reading the newspaper.

    Teacher: Right. So do you believe we could compare the television accounts with radio and newspaper accounts?

    Has the teacher used prompting effectively? Explain your answer:

_____

_____

_____

_____

_____

_____

6. Consider this interaction:

    Teacher: Arthur, has the United Nations achieved its goals?

    Arthur: I'm not sure.

    Teacher: Well, what was one of its goals?

    Arthur: To prevent war.

    Teacher: Yes, that's right Arthur. Now Barbara, have they accomplished their goal?

    Is this successful probing? Explain your answer.

_____

_____

_____

_____

_____

_____

develop an adequate answer. He redirected the question too
soon.

Answer key: 1 c, 2 a, 3 b, 4 a, 5. The teacher did not use
probing successfully. Although he posed a prompting question,
he did not allow the pupil to work towards the answer. Rather,
he answered the question himself. 6. This probing sequence is
not successful because the teacher did not allow the pupils to
develop an adequate answer. He redirected the question too
soon

Exercise 5.4

Prepare a microlesson lasting ten or fifteen minutes in which you will
practise three probing skills: prompting, seeking further clarification and
refocusing. Prepare specific questions appropriate to the skills you will
use.

Prompting should be used when a pupil says 'I don't know' or 'I can't
explain' in response to your questions. When you prompt, give the pupil
a hint, or ask one or more simple factual questions that you feel he can
answer.

You should seek further clarification when the pupil gives an answer
that you feel can be improved. This can be done by saying something
like: 'Can you explain your answer?', 'What else can you think of?', 'Tell
me more.'

Refocusing occurs when you ask a pupil to relate his reply to your
question to another previously studied topic. Refocusing questions often
start with such phrase as 'How does this relate to . . .?' or 'Can you find
a parallel between this and something we talked about yesterday?'

Do not overlook situations where more than one probing skill is called
for to help the pupil arrive at an acceptable answer.

Selection of pupils

For this lesson, you should select from your classes five pupils
who have difficulty in expressing their knowledge and ideas.

Arrange to audio-record your microlesson.

A planning supplement follows which will help you in
planning this lesson, step by step.

Planning supplement

To help you plan the lesson, complete the following questions.

1. What topic will you use for the lesson? Some suggested topics
   are:
   (a) The comparison of life in 1878 and 1978.
   (b) The various interpretations of a mythical tale that is
       part of the pupils' reading curriculum.
   (c) The duties of Parliament.

(d) The differences between, ice, water and steam.

You may select one of these topics or name one of your own. Be sure you select a topic about which you can ask several thought-provoking questions which require complex responses and not simply rote memory.

Name the topic you have selected: _____

_____

2. It is important to consider the thought-provoking questions you will ask about the topic. You should also decide before the lesson what you will accept as an adequate response to each question. List four thought-provoking questions you will ask.

(a) _____

_____

(b) _____

_____

(c) _____

_____

(d) _____

_____

For each of these questions list the ideas a pupil must include in his answer in order for it to be satisfactory.

(a) _____

_____

(b) _____

_____

(c) _____

_____

(d) _____

_____

3. In order that pupils might arrive at the same answers you have listed above, do you need to review any content with them? If so, list two related-facts questions you could use for content review. Remember to redirect these questions to several pupils.

(a) _____

_____

(b) _____

_____

4. Prompting is one of the skills you are to practise in this microlesson. Review the thought-provoking and related-facts questions you think will be most difficult for the pupils. Write at least three prompts you could use to help a pupil answer this question. (Refer back to step 2 of this plan for major ideas you want pupils to arrive at.)

(a) _____

_____

(b) _____

_____

(c) _____

_____

Select one of the related-facts questions. List two prompts you could use if a pupil gives an 'I don't know' response to the question.

(a) _____

_____

(b) _____

_____

5. Select another of the thought-provoking questions you listed earlier (do not use the same question as in step 4 above). What sort of answers might pupils give that will require further clarification? List three answers you would want clarified and what you would say to seek the clarification.

Possible pupil answers that would require clarification   *What you would say to seek clarification of the answer*

(a) _____   _____

_____   _____

(b) _____   _____

_____   _____

(c) _____   _____

_____   _____

6. Review the ideas you have listed as representing adequate responses to your thought-provoking questions (step 2). Which of the sets of ideas can best be refocused (related to other topics)? List four refocusing questions you could ask after your pupils provide satisfactory responses to your original questions. Refocusing questions:

(a) _____

_____

(b) _____

_____

(c) _____

_____

(d) _____

_____

7. Try to conduct the lesson so that you spend at least seven to eight minutes on the thought-provoking questions and the prompting, clarification, and refocusing of them. Spend as little time as possible on the related facts review.

Lesson plan form 5.4

Objective: To use probing skills to guide a pupil to more complete and thoughtful responses.

Organizational   focus: _____

_____

Planned questions	Criteria	Notes for probing
One _____	_____	_____
_____	_____	_____
_____	_____	_____
_____	_____	_____
Two _____	_____	_____
_____	_____	_____
_____	_____	_____
_____	_____	_____
_____	_____	_____

Three _____ _____ _____

_____ _____ _____

_____ _____ _____

_____ _____ _____

Four _____ _____ _____

_____ _____ _____

_____ _____ _____

_____ _____ _____

Five _____ _____ _____

_____ _____ _____

_____ _____ _____

_____ _____ _____

_____ _____ _____

Evaluation 1 (Exercise 5.4)

Purpose: To help you evaluate your use of probing techniques.

Procedure for recording observations
Play the recording of your microlesson 5.4 and record your observations on your use of probing techniques.

A probing sequence consists of a series of questions addressed to one pupil in order to improve his initial response. It is terminated when the original question is abandoned or redirected.

When a pupil response is followed by a probe, place a dot (.)

in the apropriate box to indicate whether it was a prompt, a request for further clarification or a refocusing question.

If more than one probe is used in a sequence place additional dots in the appropriate boxes (note example). Rate the last response in the sequence by ticking Unacceptable, Partially acceptable or Acceptable.

Appraisal guide: Probing techniques

Probing Sequence		Ex.	1	2	3	4	5	6	7	8	9	10	11	12	13	14	15	TOTAL
Probes	Prompt	••																
	Clarification	•																
	Refocusing																	
Terminal rating	Unacceptable																	
	Partially acceptable																	
	Acceptable																	

Comments

Interpretation

A. If a given probing sequence fails to terminate in an acceptable response, and probing is abandoned after relatively few questions, analyse that sequence for the following possible causes:

1. Your prompts may be asking the pupil to make too many big conceptual jumps. Try asking more questions requiring graduated conceptual jumps.
2. More than one prompt or request for clarification may be required.

B. If your record indicates acceptable responses but a low incidence of prompts, or an absence of clarification, determine whether you are:

1. Asking questions which do not require probing skills. You

    may be placing too much emphasis on the recall of facts instead of on thoughtful responses.

2. Not using a criterion response. This could lead to accepting any initial response.

C. If you are failing to refocus any acceptable responses you are not helping pupils develop relationships and generalize their learning to other appropriate topics. This could result from:
  1. Failure to clearly identify significant ideas in your planning which will help the pupil to form relationships in his learning.
  2. Not being sensitive to pupil responses which can usefully be used to explain related phenomena.

D. Are you using verbal rewards to reinforce acceptable responses and help pupils discriminate between acceptable and unacceptable responses?

Evaluation 2 (Exercise 5.4)

Purpose: To help you identify instances of failure to probe; replay microlesson 5.4 concentrating on instances of non-probing in the recording.

Procedure for recording observations

During the viewing, record instances when probing was not used and determine whether a probe would have been more appropriate than the teacher response used. After each instance where a pupil was not probed, record your rating of the response by ticking the appropriate box. If you feel that the response could have been probed, indicate whether you should have used a prompt, clarification or refocus question, by ticking the appropriate box.

Appraisal guide: Probing

Non-probing instance		1	2	3	4	5	6	7	8	9	10	11	12	13	14	15
	Unacceptable															
Rating	Partially acceptable															
	Acceptable															

	Prompt														
Possible probe	Clarification														
	Refocus														

Comments

Interpretation

A clear interpretation requires some comparison with the results of your first replay.

If your comparison indicates that there are more unacceptable responses followed by a failure to prompt than those which are prompted, you may be pacing your lesson too fast for your pupils or you may be including many questions which are of marginal value to the development of your lesson.
Decrease your pace or be more selective about your questions.

If your tally indicates non-probing instances where a request for clarification would be appropriate, your response criterion is not being applied. On the other hand, if you are seeking clarification, as indicated by your first viewing, your problem may be the same as that cited for failure to prompt in the previous paragraph.

Were there unused opportunities to refocus a pupil response? If there were, but you are already asking a number of refocusing questions, be sure that the ideas you are refocusing are more significant than those you are not. If you are not refocusing, more careful planning is needed.

Planning a reteach

Review your interpretation of your first and second replay to help you modify your microlesson in preparation for teaching it to a second group of five pupils. Incorporate changes suggested by the first viewings.

Improving the amount and quality of pupils' participation

Redirection

In using the technique of redirection, the same question is directed to several pupils. The question is neither repeated nor rephrased even though more than one pupil responds.

To use redirection effectively, you must choose a question which calls for an answer of related facts or allows a variety of alternative responses.

Examples: 'The police in our town carry out many duties. How many can you list? John, can you name one?'
'What were the arguments for and against our joining the European Economic Community?'
'What do you feel is the most exciting part of the story?'
'What might happen if water became a scarce resource?'

A poor question for redirection is one requiring only a single answer, such as 'What is the capital of France?' In this case, the first correct response effectively shuts off further questioning.

In order to use redirection effectively, many teachers must also correct a tendency to repeat or rephrase the question for each pupil. Unless you avoid this practice, redirection will not materially reduce your participation.

One way to handle the problem is to tell the class beforehand what you are planning to do: 'I am going to call on some of you to answer a question that has more than one answer.' Verbal prompts alert the pupils to what you are trying to do and what you expect of them.

After the pupil has supplied one of the alternatives, you should be able to obtain another to respond by simply calling his name or nodding in his direction. When you first use redirection, however, you may have to elaborate, e.g. 'Jan can you add anything else?' But these more elaborate cues can soon be dispensed with. Thus, what has been shown to be the typical pattern of question–answer, question–answer, in virtually all classrooms investigated (Bellack et al. 1966), is replaced by that of question–answer–cue–answer–cue–answer (Perrott et al. 1975).

The first result of redirection is that you will talk less and the pupils will participate more. A second gain, which can be used to advantage later, is that by requiring several pupils to respond to the same question you can begin encouraging pupils to respond to each other. One way to effect this is through such comments as, 'Tom, what do you think of Bill's answer?' and 'John, can you add anything else to Mary's answer?' In most situations, the pupils do not respond to each other (Bellack et al. 1966). The reason is not difficult to understand – pupils have been conditioned to respond to the teacher rather than to each other. It should be emphasized that when you ask a pupil to comment on another pupil's answer, your evaluation must be based on how well the answer is related to the first pupil's response.

Questions calling for sets of related facts

You undoubtedly encounter pupils in your classes who respond to almost any type of question as briefly as possible; that is, they answer 'yes' or 'no', or use only short phrases. Since most teachers ask far too many questions requiring short answers (Floyd 1966), it is easy to see how this behaviour by pupils becomes so firmly established.

Before you blame the pupils for not achieving more, be sure you are not at fault. You may be using types of questions associated with short answers that are not recognizable by their stem. One such type is the yes/no question. When you ask, 'Isn't the purpose of your local police force the protection of life and property?' you are actually seeking a simple 'yes' or 'no' response. The question is so phrased that confirmation by the pupil is an acceptable answer. If on the other hand, you want discussion, you should phrase the same questions as follows: 'What are the duties of our local police force?' A 'yes' or 'no' response will not suffice here (Groisser 1964).

Another variant is a little more subtle. In this instance the teacher appears to be calling for a long response, but the question is so phrased that a brief answer will suffice. An example would be, 'Why does the less careful consumer buy strictly by brand name?' The same question might have been asked in another way, 'What are the advantages and disadvantages of buying strictly by brand name?' Remember you can often avoid poor questions by preparing them before class and framing the probable answers.

But what if you have good questions and the pupils are still not responding adequately? Where do you start? As we have suggested, the question itself is only part of the story. Pupils previously allowed to respond briefly or to give memory-type responses are not likely to respond to your expectations at first. For example when you say, 'What are some of the duties of our mayor?' the response may not approach what you ultimately would like in the way of longer responses. Here is where you begin training your pupils.

You should definitely not punish pupils who give correct but short or conceptually simple answers to questions designed to elicit longer answers. Praise the pupil for what he has stated and ask him to contribute more. Success lies in using questions which require longer and better responses and in reinforcing the pupils for their successively longer and better responses.

Higher-order questions

Besides encouraging pupils to give longer responses you should also try to improve the quality of their responses.

The kinds of questions the teacher asks will reveal to the pupil the kind of thinking which is expected of him. Since different kinds of questions stimulate different kinds of thinking, the teacher must be conscious of the purpose of his questions and the level of thinking they evoke.

An effective questioning sequence is one that achieves its purpose.

A. When your purpose is to determine whether pupils remember certain specific facts, ask recall questions.

Examples: What is the capital of Canada?

When did Henry VIII become King of England?

Name two kinds of blood-vessels in the body.

B. When your purpose is to require pupils to use information in order to either summarize, compare, contrast, explain, analyse, synthesize or evaluate ask higher-order questions. (see p 48)

Examples: Explain in your own words the kinds of problems caused by unemployment.

How did life in the eighteenth century differ from life today?

What is your opinion of abstract art?

Exercise 5.5

Prepare a microlesson lasting approximately ten minutes which will enable you to increase the amount and quality of pupils' participation while decreasing your own participation by practising:
1. Redirection.
2. Asking questions which call for sets of related facts.
3. Asking higher-order questions.
Arrange for an audio-recording to be made of your lesson.

A planning supplement follows which will help you prepare your microlesson step by step.

Planning supplement

To help you plan the lesson, complete the following questions:

1. What topic will you use for the microlesson?
   Some suggested topics are:
   (a) A government or commercial agency such as a public transport system or the police department.
   (b) A current event that has received extensive coverage by the media.
   (c) The living habits of two animals, which differ considerably.

   You could select one of these topics or name one of your own, but be sure to select a topic that has many features that can be discussed.

   Name the topic you have selected: _____

   _____

2. In this lesson you are to practise asking higher-order questions, redirecting questions to several pupils and framing questions that call for longer responses from pupils. Use higher-order questions to help pupils develop more complex ideas about the topic you have chosen.

   For example, some higher-order questions for the topic (a) listed above might be:

Type of higher-order question	Example
Comprehension (summarize)	Tell us what you know about travel by train or aeroplane.
(comparison)	Compare travel by aeroplane with travel by train.
(explanation)	Why do trains run according to schedule?
Application	Using the railway map we have just studied, name the city to which it is easiest to travel to from any part of the country.
Analysis	Why are some cities better served by rail than others?
Synthesis	How could the railway system in

Evaluation

Britain be improved?
Which is the better way to travel
to Paris, by train or by car?

Review the topic you have selected for your microlesson. List
three higher-order questions you will ask your pupils.
Remember, you can ask questions that ask pupils to: compare,
contrast, explain, summarize, synthesize, evaluate. Use three
different types of questions.

Questions to be asked   **Type of question**

(a) _____   _____

_____

(b) _____   _____

_____

(c) _____   _____

_____

3. What must be included in a pupil's answer before it is
   acceptable? Write a criterion response for each question.

   (a) _____

   _____

   (b) _____

   _____

   (c) _____

   _____

4. Start this lesson by redirecting several related-facts or
   multiple-opinion questions that will help the pupils bring
   together the content they will need to respond to the
   higher-order questions. Examples of related-fact and
   multiple-opinion questions (for one of the above topics) are:

Related facts

What are the different jobs that people do in the transport system?

Multiple opinion

If you could go from London to Edinburgh by any form of transport you wished, what kind would you choose?

Consider the higher-order questions you have just planned.

(a) What content do you want to be sure the pupils know? _____

_____

_____

(b) List two related-fact questions you will ask and then redirect to several pupils to be sure they know the content.

(1) _____

_____

(2) _____

_____

(c) List two multiple-opinion questions you will ask about the content.

(1) _____

_____

(2) _____

_____

5. Since the microlesson is only ten minutes in length, try to conduct the lesson so that you spend the first two to three minutes on the initial related-fact and multiple-opinion questions. Spend seven to eight minutes on the higher-order questions. Remember to encourage pupils to respond to each other, by positive reactions such as smiling or nodding when this occurs.

6. Now that you have planned your questions, organize them for

teaching on the lesson plan form below.

Lesson plan form 5.5

Objective: To ask higher-order questions; use redirection and frame questions which increase the quantity and quality of pupil responses.

Organizational focus: _____

_____

Initial questions (remember to redirect)	**Criteria**
One _____	_____
_____	_____
Two _____	_____
_____	_____
Three _____	_____
_____	_____
Four _____	_____

Higher-order questions	**Criteria**
One _____	_____
_____	_____
Two _____	_____
_____	_____
Three _____	_____
_____	_____

Notes

Evaluation 1 (Exercise 5.5)

Purpose: To help you evaluate your use of redirection.

Procedure for recording observations
Replay the recording of your microlesson and note your
observations as shown in the table below. Stop or replay recording
if necessary. Each sequence of redirection is numbered
consecutively in the table below. During each redirection sequence
place a dot (.) in the corresponding box for each pupil to whom
the question is redirected after the first pupil has answered. A
redirection sequence is terminated when a new question is asked.

Appraisal guide: Redirection

Sequence	Ex.	1	2	3	4	5	6	7	8	9	10	11	12	13	14	15	TOTAL
Number of pupils involved	• ••																

Comments

Interpretation

Redirection is intended to reduce the amount of the teacher's
verbal participation and to increase pupil participation.

Are you using redirection to increase the quantity of pupil
participation? Note the number of redirection sequences which
occur, but particularly note the number of pupils involved in
individual redirection sequences. The number of pupils involved
in each questioning sequence should increase as you gain more
skill. Check to see if your individual questions really allow for
several pupils to participate.

Evaluation 2 (Exercise 5.5)

Purpose: To help you evaluate your use of higher-order
questions.

Procedure for recording observations

Replay the recording of your microlesson and note your
observations as shown below. Stop and replay sections of the
tape where necessary for accurate categorization.

After each question put a dot (.) in the appropriate square to
classify it as recall or higher-order. Do not classify rhetorical
questions or procedural questions, e.g. 'Have you read the
story?' After each pupil response, use a dot to classify the
answer in the corresponding box. Multiple pupil responses to
redirection should be shown as in the example on the form.
Circle dots to indicate pupil to pupil interaction.

Intent of teacher questions	Ex.	1	2	3	4	5	6	7	8	9	10	11	12	13	14	15	TOTAL
Recall																	
Higher-order	•																
Level of pupil response	Ex.	1	2	3	4	5	6	7	8	9	10	11	12	13	14	15	TOTAL
Recall	•																
Higher-order	•																

Comments

Interpretation

A. Are you using higher-order questions to improve the quality
   of pupils' responses? A preponderance of dots in the recall
   columns would indicate that you are emphasizing rote
   memory. If this is so, try to plan so that a larger percentage
   of your questions require the manipulation of information.

B. Are pupils responding to your higher-order questions with higher-order answers? If they are not:
   1. Do you understand the differences which discriminate between remembering information and manipulating information?
   2. Do your questions require higher-order responses?
   If you find any difficulty ask a colleague or your supervisor to join you in replaying and scoring your microlesson. After evaluation compare the two evaluations. If there are differences of interpretation discuss the possible causes.
      Also answer the following questions.

C. Are you using redirection to increase the quality of pupil participation? If most of the questions which you redirect call for sets of related facts, you have gained little by increasing the quantity of participation while maintaining thought at the recall level. Use redirection at the recall level only in so far as is necessary to determine that the pupils know information essential to the development of higher-order answers.

D. Are you encouraging pupils to respond to each other? Discussion skills can be developed by encouraging pupils to respond to each other and initiate questions.

Developing a questioning strategy

The primary objective of this chapter has been to help you acquire and use questioning skills which can be used to improve the quality and quantity of pupil participation. Consistent with this goal, you have been asked to evaluate your microteaching performance in terms of the extent to which you are using a particular set of skills. But, as you read previously, the use of skills is a means to an end, not an end in itself. The question of whether the use of a particular skill is 'good' or 'bad' is the wrong question. The important question is 'Good for what?'

   In order to be effective, skills must be appropriately incorporated into a questioning strategy planned to achieve particular learning objectives.

   To a large extent, the ability to use a skill appropriately is dependent upon a clear awareness of its function. Failure to be aware of these functions can result in an inappropriate use of skills.

The following summary indicates the relationships between functions and skills.

Function	Skill	Participant
To increase readiness to respond	Pausing Handling incorrect responses Calling on non-volunteers	Class Individual Individual
To increase quantity of participation	Redirecting questions Calling for sets of related facts	Class
To improve quality of response	Asking higher-order questions Prompting Seeking clarification Refocusing	Individual Individual Individual Individual
To increase quantity of participation while improving quality of response	Redirecting higher-order questions	Class

Problems in questioning sequences

1. A common problem in questioning sequences is a lack of emphasis on higher-order questions. This may be due to failure in planning a strategy where the primary objective is the improvement of the quality of thought. In part it may also be related to the fact that questioning is taking place in a group situation where the teacher is concerned with the quantity of pupil participation. In his effort to increase the quantity of pupil participation a teacher might rely on redirecting a disproportionate number of multiple-fact questions. Such tactics tend to emphasize recall and decrease the time available for asking higher-order questions and probing.

The teacher who is conscious of this dilemma can ameliorate the situation by a well-balanced use of skills. Careful planning will enable him to ask questions requiring the recall of facts only when they are necessary as a preliminary to higher-order questions, while the conscious effort to redirect higher-order questions will result in an improvement of the quality as well as the quantity of participation.

2. Another common problem relates to the teacher's failure to refocus. A primary task of the teacher is to help pupils relate

what they are presently learning to what they have previously learned. Perhaps an even more significant task is to help pupils to understand that the ideas which they are studying are often relevant to other situations. Refocusing is probably the most difficult probing skill. Although the use of this skill depends on the preceding answer of the pupil, teachers who have clearly in mind the conceptual content of their lesson can plan for questioning sequences which enable them to use refocusing.

3. A third problem arises from the teacher's failure to have clearly in mind criteria for evaluating pupil responses. As previously mentioned, skills provide a means to an end. Only by specifying a particular end can a teacher determine which means are appropriate.

Summary

To help your pupils develop skills in higher-order thinking, your questioning strategy should move through two phases. The initial phase should consist of a brief review of the relevant facts the pupil needs to know. Recall questions serve a useful function in this early part of a questioning period. The actual point at which your higher-order questioning sequence begins depends on the responses you obtain to your preliminary questions.

In planning a discussion, remember that recall questions should be asked only in so far as they are necessary for the development of higher-order questions. Also, there is only marginal value in increasing the number of pupils responding, if the majority of their answers remain at recall level.

To increase the quality of pupils' answers teachers should:
1. Carefully plan questions which require higher-order responses.
2. Have in mind the criteria for an acceptable answer.
3. Identify previously learned facts which are essential to the initiation of the higher-order questions.
4. Review for essential information to determine what the pupils know.
5. Frame questions that can be used systematically to develop the original pupil response and meet the criteria.

Additional reading

Perrott, E., Applebee, A. N., Watson, E. and Heap, B. (1975)
Effective Questioning – a self-instructional microteaching course.
(3 vols – Teachers Handbook, Co-ordinator's Guide and Evaluation

Manual; and 5 films or videotapes), Guild Sound and Vision, Peterborough. This is a fifteen-hour self-instructional course requiring study of the written materials, the viewing of other teachers using the questioning skills being studied, practice sessions of microteaching and the evaluation of practice.

Chapter 6
Affective communication in the classroom

Researchers have found that feelings are seldom acknowledged verbally in the classroom (Amidon and Hough 1967). But it is important that teachers should not ignore the significant emotional content of what pupils are saying and doing any more than they would ignore important cognitive statements.

The teacher's task is to promote interest and learning. Success in promoting interest is communicated to the teacher by numbers of non-verbal cues. Lively, interested pupils usually sit with heads slightly forward and turned towards the teacher. (Fig. 6.1) Their eyes are wide open and a few of them will sometimes be

Fig. 6.1 A lively, interested pupil.

obviously waiting for a chance to speak. (Fig. 6.2)
On the other hand, bored pupils often slouch and turn slightly
away from the teacher. Their faces are expressionless and their
eyelids may be partially closed. (Fig. 6.3) Some pupils may be

Fig. 6.2　A partly attentive class.

Fig. 6.3　A bored class.

fidgeting, running their fingers through their hair or furtively communicating with each other. It is important to monitor your classes for these signs when you are teaching. It will help you to anticipate when a change of activity or a break is required and is an important element in classroom control (Kounin 1970).

Exercise 6.1

Arrange for a ten-minute microlesson, which includes exposition and discussion, to be videotaped with the camera focused on both teacher and pupils (see Fig. 3.1). When viewing the video-recording pay particular attention to cues of interest or boredom given by pupils. Relate these to your teaching behaviour.

It is important to remember that the teacher is also sending out verbal and non-verbal affective messages as well as receiving them. The teacher who talks to the class in a dull monotonous voice, and as he talks looks at the floor is sending two kinds of affective cues – verbal and non-verbal – to his class. Since communication is both verbal and non-verbal, actions often speak louder than words. In fact, through their researches, Mehrabian and Weiner (1966) have determined that over 90 per cent of the messages teachers send their pupils are non-verbal.

An important aspect of most teacher–pupil interaction is eliciting pupils' expressions of feeling. Through the use of various non-verbal and verbal cues, the teacher can demonstrate that he is listening with care and empathy to what is being said to him. Consequently, he can encourage pupils to share their thoughts and feelings with him and know that they are being heard (Argyle 1970).

Effective attending behaviour

Listed below are suggestions for developing effective attending behaviour

(a) Non-verbal cues

    (i)   *Eye contact.* Focus your eyes directly on the speaker.

    (ii) *Facial expressions.* Your expression can provide feedback to the speaker, prompting him to say more, or to slow down. More important, let your facial expression encourage the speaker. But beware of too much expression, especially negative expression. It is

important that you be aware of your own facial
expressions and the effect they have on the pupils.

(iii) *Body posture.* Body gestures also communicate meaning.
For instance, when a listener leans toward the speaker, a
high level of interest is communicated.

(iv) *Physical space.* The distance people create between
themselves has an inherent communication value
(Hall 1966). Find a comfortable space between yourself
and your class.

(b) Verbal cues

Many teachers feel compelled to make an immediate response
and begin searching for a reply before a pupil has concluded
speaking. Wait a few seconds to be sure a pupil has finished
what he has to say. It gives a chance for reflection on what has
been said and often encourages the pupil to say more. On the
other hand, nothing is more deadly than an inappropriate
silence. If you feel it is required, brief verbal reactions such as
'yes' or 'I see' will let the speaker know you are listening without
interrupting. But keep reactions brief and quickly refocus on the
speaker.

Exercise 6.2

Plan a ten-minute microlesson, which includes discussion and arrange
for it to be videotaped with the camera focused on both the teacher and
pupils (see Fig. 3.1). When viewing the video-recording pay particular
attention to both the non-verbal and the verbal cues you gave the
pupils. Relate these cues to pupil's reactions. If you are unable to
arrange for a video recording, make an audio-recording and ask a
colleague or your supervisor to observe your lesson and complete the
appraisal guide. Listen to the audio-recording and complete the appraisal
guide. Then discuss with your colleague or supervisor.

The need for active listening

Silence and brief verbal acknowledgements have limitations in
some circumstances, because they are passive and do not provide
much interaction. The pupil is doing all the work. In addition
the pupil has no way of knowing if the teacher understands; he
only knows that the teacher is listening. Effective listening often
requires more interaction and proof that the teacher has
understood accurately. This type of response has been called
active listening.

For *active listening* to be effective the teacher must think with the pupil, not ahead of his pupil. He is neither anticipating, judging nor analysing, by drawing conclusions before the pupil has concluded and he is not thinking for the pupil, by trying to find solutions to problems before the pupil has concluded. Effective listening requires the teacher: (a) to be aware of and to put aside preconceived expectations; (b) to attend carefully to both the pupil's verbal and non-verbal cues in order to differentiate between the cognitive content and the emotional content being transmitted.

Reinforcement

Reinforcement or the reward of desirable pupil behaviour is a frequently used teaching skill. Here are some examples:

A pupil gives a good answer to which the teacher responds by saying 'very good', or 'excellent'.

A pupil is telling you about an experience. You smile, look animated and lean forward. But although reinforcement is so frequently used it is only during the last decade that extensive studies have been made on its use in the classroom. The evidence produced by these studies indicates that various aspects of praise and corrective feedback are positively correlated with pupil's achievement and positive attitudes (Flanders and Simon 1969; Rosenshine 1971).

Reinforcement techniques fall into two main categories: verbal and non-verbal.

(a) Verbal reinforcement

The most common verbal reinforcers are the one-word or brief phrase responses, e.g. 'good', 'splendid', or 'well done'. Praise not only changes behaviour, it develops confidence and a positive self-image. A pupil who is weak academically and lacks confidence may need considerable help and praise, while a clever and confident pupil may not need so much positive reinforcement. There are, however, a number of other reinforcers which are less frequently used, yet can provide pupils with powerful rewards. An important type of reinforcement, but one used less than 10 per cent of the time occurs when the teacher responds to the ideas pupils express by accepting them, summarizing them, applying them, building on them or asking

questions based on them (Flanders 1970; Rosenshine 1971).
For example:

Teacher: What kind of mammal would it be feasible for us to keep in the laboratory?

John: I think mice would be best.

Teacher: Would you repeat your suggestion John, so that everyone can hear. (Accepting)

John: I think mice would be best.

Susan: I think hamsters would be more interesting.

Teacher: Do you mean that hamsters are more instructive? (Asking question for clarification)

Susan: Yes.

Teacher: Mice and hamsters have been suggested. How can we decide between them?

It has been shown that in classes where such reinforcement techniques are applied, pupils have more positive attitudes and higher achievement than in classrooms where pupils' ideas are not incorporated into the development of lessons. Such verbal reinforcement can be a powerful motive for increasing a pupil's desire to participate.

(b) Non-verbal reinforcement

Several research studies indicate that non-verbal reinforcement may in fact be even more powerful than verbal reinforcement. Non-verbal reinforcement refers to the physical messages sent by teachers through cues such as eye contact, facial expressions and body position. Does the teacher smile, frown or remain impassive when a pupil responds in class discussion? Where is the teacher standing? Does the teacher appear relaxed or tense? All these non-verbal messages indicate to the pupil whether the teacher is interested or bored, involved or passive. A smile, or nod of the head and friendly eye contact can be used to encourage participation. But often praise is a mixture of verbal and non-verbal reinforcement, e.g. the nod and friendly eye contact being accompanied by the phrase 'well done'.

But reinforcement is not always an effective teaching skill. In some cases it is ineffectual and on occasion, actually detrimental to learning. For instance, when a teacher relies totally on one or two favourite types of reinforcement and uses these reinforcers repeatedly, the eventual result may be that the teacher's attempts at reinforcement become ineffectual. A teacher who, for example, continually says 'good' after each pupil response is not reinforcing, but simply verbalizing a comment that has lost its power to reward. In such cases the continual repetition of 'good' is probably only easing the teacher's anxiety or providing him with a second or two to think of his next comment or question.

Some teachers, fearful of discouraging pupils, use reinforcement indiscriminately, thus sacrificing critical thinking and accuracy for the sake of goodwill. It is important to remember that a teacher can reward pupil participation, e.g. 'that was a good attempt' and still indicate that the response was not entirely appropriate, e.g. 'remember now, we are concentrating on the difficulties experienced by scientists at the moment. Can someone tackle the question again, keeping this in mind?' Rewarding answers indiscriminately is an example of an inappropriate use of reinforcement, but rewarding a good effort is possible even when the answer is incorrect.

Again, reinforcement given too quickly may interfere with the complete development of a pupil's ideas. During problem-solving activities reinforcement may actually terminate problem-solving altogether. Reinforcement can also interfere with pupil-to-pupil interactions. A teacher who reacts to each pupil comment is refocusing the discussion on himself. Another inhibitor of pupil to pupil interaction is direct eye contact, which also tends to refocus attention on the teacher.

However, the use of reinforcement is not confined to discussion or question and answer sessions. Reinforcement may also be used by the teacher to regulate other types of behaviour. For instance, praising an untidy pupil who on a rare occasion produces a well-presented exercise, will encourage him to keep up the improvement. Praising a group after they have successfully completed a difficult assignment, or complimenting an individual on his diligence can produce a glow of satisfaction. Using pupils' names in a friendly manner and showing interest in them as individuals contributes to promoting a happy, friendly class which is ready to work.

Finally, it should be pointed out that different individuals respond to different kinds of reinforcement. For instance, some pupils find intensive eye contact rewarding while others find it uncomfortable. Although it is unrealistic to expect that you will be able to learn the type of reinforcement to which every pupil responds best, it is possible for you to try, in general, to be sensitive to the effects of different types of reinforcement on different pupils.

Exercise 6.3

1. Plan a microlesson of approximately ten minutes' duration which involves questions and answers and pupil discussion. Arrange for it to be videotaped with the camera focused on both yourself and the pupils (see Fig. 3.1).
2. Teach the microlesson using as many examples of both verbal and non-verbal reinforcement as possible.
3. Study the appraisal guide given below.
4. View your lesson and assess your performance by using the appraisal guide.
5. If you are unable to arrange for a video-recording, make an audio-recording and ask a colleague or your supervisor to observe and complete the appraisal guide. Listen to the audio-recording and complete the appraisal guide. Then discuss with your colleague or supervisor.

Evaluation (Exercise 6.3)

VTR Operation: Start tape at beginning and record your observations as directed below. Stop and replay the tape if necessary.

Sample: Entire tape.

Procedure for recording observations
At each instance of reinforcement used, place a tick in the appropriate box to classify it according to the descriptions on the left.

Appraisal guide: Reinforcement

Types of reinforcement	Number of instances		
	1 2 3 4 5 6 7 8 9 10 11 12	TOTAL	
1. *Positive verbal comments* e.g. 'good', 'excellent', 'well done'			
2. *Positive gestures or facial expressions* Encouraged pupils to participate by using cues such as nodding of head, smiling			
3. *Accepts pupils' ideas* Acknowledges pupil's			

contributions by 'yes', or 'I see', asking a pupil to repeat for the benefit of the class, summarizing pupil's contribution		
4. *Builds on or asks questions on pupils' ideas*		
5. *Rewarding pupils who give partially correct answers*, e.g. 'a good attempt but look again carefully', and avoiding negative comments or gestures		

Comments

Interpretation

If your record indicates a low incidence of reinforcement, replay your tape with a view to identifying instances when reinforcement could have been used.

1. Are you using sufficient non-verbal reinforcement?
2. Are you using verbal rewards to reinforce acceptable responses?
3. Are you sensitive to pupils' responses which can be built upon in the lesson?

Reteach the microlesson you have prepared to another group, bearing these points in mind and compare your evaluation of it with your original attempt.

Using criticism

There are times when a pupil's answer is wrong and he must be corrected. We are emphasizing here criticism of the response, not of the person. However, most pupils take criticism more or less personally. If you indicate that you are concerned with the answer as separate and different from the pupil, you can avoid much resentment, withdrawal and other problems.

Technically speaking, punishment is any aversive consequence following a response. In the usual classroom discussion, the most frequent punishment pattern is an incorrect pupil's response followed by a negative comment, for example, telling the pupil, 'you're wrong', or showing irritation by frowning, saying 'no' and calling on another pupil to give the answer, e.g. 'Keith – you tell him'.

As a teacher you probably feel ambivalènt about punishment. You want to tell the pupil his response is wrong, but you know you are likely to hurt his feelings. Punishment is a form of special interaction (Millenson 1967) and the effects on both the teacher and pupil must be taken into consideration. Sometimes the immediate effects of punishment on a pupil are to make him pause or change his answer immediately. On the other hand, because the pupil's undesired behaviour ceases, the teacher's punishing behaviour is reinforced. It can be argued that a pupil's incorrect response is aversive to most teachers, reflecting, perhaps, on their effectiveness. The teaching behaviour that stops the pupil, i.e. telling the pupil he is wrong, is thereby strengthened because the preceding pupil behaviour, the incorrect response, is terminated. In short, any response on your part which stops something that is aversive to you is likely to be repeated. Moreover, punishment not only has the short-range consequences cited above, but may also have long-lasting effects. Here are some examples:

1. Punishment does not necessarily eradicate undesirable behaviour by pupils. Under certain circumstances, once punishment is withdrawn the behaviour will be repeated.
2. Punishment often generates emotional reactions, for example, anxiety, hate, fear, which have long-lasting consequences. These emotional responses are likely to be associated with the teacher, classroom and/or the entire learning situation. Subsequently, the pupil may display behaviour ranging from refusing to answer questions and sulking to playing truant and outright defiance of the teacher.
3. The pupil will also do things which serve to reduce future possibility of punishment. For example, if he is punished for an incorrect answer to a question, he may subsequently refuse to volunteer answers in class.

But to repeat a point made earlier, you must let the pupil know when his answer is incorrect. One solution that achieves this, but that still avoids many problems of punishment is probing, which involves working with the pupil to obtain a more desirable answer. Probing skills are fully discussed in Chapter 5. However, there are occasions when you may feel it necessary to tell the pupil directly that his answer is incorrect. There are several procedures you may use to mitigate some of the reactions to this kind of punishment.

First, you should be aware that a given negative verbal statement will not have equal consequences for all pupils (Krasner 1958). When you say, 'that answer is wrong', the statement may be mildly aversive to one pupil and extremely aversive to another. The solution, as some teachers see it, is to tell a pupil that his answer is incorrect in a way that keeps him interested in the discussion and does not cut off future participation.

To do this, you must become sensitive to the pupil's reaction. Again, nothing is better than looking and listening. You can accomplish your aims by observing carefully the behaviour of the pupil after he has been told his answer was incorrect. Suppose you tell a pupil his answer is wrong. Subsequently he exhibits a great deal of emotional behaviour, for example, he sulks and does not raise his hand for the remainder of the period. You may conclude that he reacts rather strongly to failure and some precautionary steps should be taken; these will be discussed shortly.

A second alternative is for you to tell a pupil that his answer was incorrect and then provide him with an opportunity for an alternative response that can be accepted, i.e. reinforced. In other words, if he has given an incorrect response, encourage him to take another try at answering the question.

Example: Teacher: Can you name some of Europe's major seaports, James?
Pupil: Paris.
Teacher: No, not Paris, try again.
Pupil: Rotterdam.
Teacher: Yes, Rotterdam, very good.
A variation of this skill is to determine if part of the answer is correct and to reinforce this part.

Example: Teacher: Can you name the causes of the Industrial Revolution?
Pupil: The invention of new machines and rebellion

of the workers.

Teacher: Yes, the invention of new machines was one
of the causes of the Industrial Revolution,
but the rebellion of the workers was not.
Can you give me any other causes?

Thus, you ask the pupil to reconsider the incorrect part only.

As indicated earlier, the best way of overcoming the problems
of punishment is to avoid any negative statements at all.
Remember, too, that verbal statements are not the only aversive
controls employed by the teacher. Sour facial expressions and
looking away from the pupil while he is responding are also
socially aversive. Basically, the teacher should omit all value
judgements, even if the response is incorrect, and instead work
with the pupils to obtain a more desirable answer, provide
opportunities for alternative answers and ask pupils to reconsider
partially incorrect answers. To summarize, you should try to be
positive in your response to the pupil's participation.

Calling on non-volunteers

The effects of non-punitive teaching behaviour in encouraging
pupils' participation can also be enhanced by calling on
non-volunteers. It is not enough to get some pupils to respond,
all pupils should participate.

As in correcting incorrect responses, the questions asked of
non-volunteers should be chosen carefully so that pupils'
contributions will be successful. Questions having a purely right
or wrong answer are generally not as useful as questions asking
for personal opinion or information based on the pupils'
experience.

The teacher should avoid practices which decrease the pupils'
participation, e.g. calling on non-volunteers should not be used
as a form of punishment for pupils who are unprepared or
inattentive. Instead the teacher should try to convey the message
that all pupils' participation is valued and sought.

The purpose of calling on non-volunteers is to:
1. Provide an opportunity for the teacher to reward
   participation by reinforcing the answers of students who are
   generally non-participants.
2. Prevent the monopolization of class discussion by a limited
   number of habitual volunteers.
3. Provide more accurate feedback of the thinking of the group
   as a whole.

Exercise 6.4

Prepare a microlesson lasting ten or fifteen minutes in which you will practise two skills.
1. Handling incorrect answers in a non-punitive manner.
2. Calling on both volunteers and non-volunteers.

You will not need specific preparation for treating incorrect answers non-punitively. But before you begin, remind yourself to be aware of the manner in which you respond to pupils' answers.

Selection of pupils

For this particular microlesson, you should select six pupils from one of your classes, about half of whom are usually non-volunteers. These pupils will provide you with the opportunity to practise calling on both volunteers and non-volunteers in order to distribute participation more evenly.

Use the lesson plan form overleaf which will help you in preparing your microlesson.

Lesson plan form

Objective: To use appropriately two skills to encourage pupil participation.

Organizational focus: _____

Planned questions	**Criteria**
One _____	_____
_____	_____
_____	_____
Two _____	_____
_____	_____
_____	_____
Three _____	_____
_____	_____
_____	_____

Four _____   _____

_____   _____

_____   _____

Five _____   _____

_____   _____

_____   _____

Notes:

Arrange to record your microlesson on videotape if possible. If this is not possible, use an audio-recording, but ask a colleague or your supervisor to observe and evaluate your microlesson for your questioning of non-volunteers.

Evaluation 1 (Exercise 6.4)

Purpose: To evaluate your handling of incorrect responses.

Procedure for recording observations
Play the entire tape. After each instance of an incorrect response make your tally. Tally the first instance of an incorrect response by the pupil under 'Incorrect pupil response' 1, the second under 2, etc. When a pupil gives an incorrect response, indicate your handling of the response by referring to the descriptions on the left and make a check mark in the appropriate box. If there were no incorrect responses, write 'none' across the appraisal guide.

Appraisal guide: Incorrect responses

Rating of teacher's responses	Incorrect pupil response									
	1	2	3	4	5	6	7	8	9	10
Provides for alternative response										
Accepts in part										
Slightly negative										

Comments

Interpretation

If you show a tendency to handle incorrect responses in a negative manner, pupils are likely to stop volunteering in class. If called on, they will tend to be as brief as possible in their responses. Aversive teaching behaviour can also lead to emotional behaviour that will interfere with general classroom management.

Planning the reteach

Now replan your original lesson in preparation for teaching it to a second group of five pupils. Incorporate changes suggested by the first viewing. It is also useful to practise a variety of techniques for responding to incorrect answers in a positive manner until they are spontaneous and feel comfortable.

Evaluation 2 (Exercise 6.4)

Purpose: To evaluate your use of calling on non-volunteers to encourage participation by all pupils.

Procedure for recording observations

A video-recording will give you the opportunity to evaluate yourself after you have given the microlesson. If it is not practicable, ask a colleague or supervisor to record their observations on the appraisal guide below, while you are giving the microlesson and to discuss it with you afterwards.

Each time a pupil is called upon, enter his initials to indicate whether he volunteered or did not volunteer. Volunteering is defined as raising a hand, etc., non-volunteering is defined as no indication that the pupil wished to take part. After each pupil response tick the appropriate box to indicate whether you reinforced the pupil's participation.

Appraisal guide: Calling on non-volunteers

Questions		1	2	3	4	5	6	7	8	9	10	Total
Pupil	Volunteer											
	Non-volunteer											
Reinforcement	Yes											
	No											

Comments:

Interpretation

Calling on non-volunteers prevents the monopolization of discussion by a few pupils and allows teachers positively to reinforce the participation of all pupils. The tallies in each pupil response column will indicate to what extent you are achieving this. If you are not satisfied, analyse your tallies for the following possible explanations:
1. Failure to call on sufficient number of non-volunteers.
2. Failure to call on sufficient number of volunteers.
3. Failure positively to reinforce participation of non-volunteers.
4. Failure to ask appropriate questions of non-volunteers.

Additional reading

Annett, J. (1969) *Feedback and Human Performance*, Penguin, Harmondsworth (esp. Ch. 1 and 7).
Argyle, M. (1967) *The Psychology of Interpersonal Behaviour*, Pelican, Harmondsworth.
Argyle, M., (1970) *Social Interaction*, Methuen, London.

Cook, M. (1971) *Interpersonal Perception*, Penguin, Harmondsworth.
Morrison, A. and McIntyre, D. eds. (1972) *Social Psychology of Teaching*, Penguin, Harmondsworth (esp. Parts 5, 6 and 7).

Chapter 7

Class organization

Many inexperienced teachers feel overwhelmed by the task of trying to manage a room full of lively pupils and the questions they commonly ask me: 'How does one keep order', 'How does one interest a class which is bored or hostile?' These are important questions and many volumes dealing with educational philosophy and educational psychology deal with the problems of class control.

Teaching consists of two major sets of activities: instruction and management. Instructional activities are intended to facilitate the pupil's achievement of specific educational objectives directly, e.g. diagnosing individual needs, presenting information, asking questions and evaluating progress. Managerial activities, on the other hand, are intended to create and maintain conditions in which instruction can take place effectively. They are the activities by which the teacher maintains a productive classroom organization.

In situations where the class works as a single unit on the same task the distinction between instructional and managerial teaching activities tends to be clear-cut and consequently managerial problems are easier to solve. But in classrooms where independent studies are organized for individuals and small groups, managerial and instructional teaching activities are closely interrelated, making managerial problems more complex.

Organizing independent studies for a full-size class

Independent studies are a feature of many classrooms, especially at the primary level and increasingly at the secondary level also. This type of organization recognizes the fact that in any class of thirty pupils there is bound to be a wide range of ability and interests and caters for them. In such classes each pupil is able to pursue agreed studies at an appropriate level, which reflect his own interests.

Independent study can include a variety of activities such as undertaking investigations in field or laboratory, interviewing people, visiting museums and factories. It may involve gathering information from a variety of sources and presenting it in the form of a report, chart or model. It may also consist of investigations which involve the analysis and evaluation of information in order to solve problems.

Although the scope of the work in an independent study should suit the needs and ability of the pupil, the choice of subject-matter will usually be restricted by the curriculum. There will also be limits to where and when the work is carried out.

Independent studies can operate successfully in a variety of different classroom environments, whether they are fundamentally open-plan, informal or formal. The main requirement is that the classroom should be arranged to suit the pupils' needs. For example, tables may be regrouped to suit individuals or small groups (Fig. 7.1) and a specific area may be set aside for practical work, such as constructing models. There are, however, other basic requirements which are essential if this type of work is to be effective.

Fig. 7.1 Independent studies in the classroom.

Many of the resources to be used by the pupils will be kept in the classroom, e.g. reference books, workbooks, pamphlets, apparatus, construction materials and collected objects. It is essential that the pupils know where these resources are kept and that they are readily accessible. There may be one or two expensive or fragile items which need to be kept on 'restricted access', but remember that every time a pupil has to see you before he or she collects resources, his or her work will be slowed down and your discussions with other pupils will be interrupted. Pupils may also need ready access to resources elsewhere in the school. How you arrange this will obviously depend on the organization of the school. Remember, however, that you cannot afford to spend too much time helping any one pupil find his resources.

While independent study caters for individual differences, it often fails to run smoothly because of the diverse demands being made on the teacher. While some pupils respond well to working independently, others will need closer supervision and will constantly demand help, advice or encouragement. If the majority of pupils make such claims, the teacher is put under great strain and finds it difficult to meet adequately such a variety of needs. There are, however, techniques which can assist the beginning teacher in avoiding this sort of situation.

You will find it helpful to assess each pupil's ability to carry out planning for an independent study before he or she actually plans it in detail. This assessment will allow you to estimate the amount of help each pupil is likely to need. You will also be able to find out which areas of his or her chosen independent study the pupil can plan competently and in which areas he or she will require guidance.

Levels of independence in planning

When you assess a pupil for his or her levels of independence in planning an independent study, carry out your assessment by discussing a piece of independent work with him or her. On the basis of this discussion, make a judgement about the pupil's levels of independence, by considering his or her ability to carry out four of the seven stages in planning an independent study. You will be concerned with the pupils' ability to:
1. Define a topic for himself.
2. Identify a number of resources.

3. Outline a series of learning steps.
4. Set realistic deadlines for the completion of his work.

As you discuss each of the four stages outlined above, make a decision about the pupil's ability to plan and classify him or her at the appropriate level of independence.

For the purpose of making a simple assessment of a pupil's ability to plan these four stages in planning an independent study, the wide range of levels of independence in pupils has been divided into three main categories: guided level, cooperative level and independent level. You should remember, however, that these are arbitrary categories on a continuum and are not discrete and easily identifiable. Also, it is quite possible that the pupil will be at different levels for the different stages.

Guided level

Classify a pupil at guided level for a particular stage if he or she responds as shown below:

(i) Topic: when questioned on his or her choice of topic the pupil offers an 'I don't know' response because he or she is not sufficiently able or experienced in independent work to suggest work he or she would like to do on his or her own.
(ii) Resources: the pupil cannot name any resources for a chosen independent study.
(iii) Learning steps: the pupil cannot outline the tasks he or she will have to carry out.
(iv) Deadlines: the pupil has no idea how long the work will take.

When a pupil is at guided level for any one of these four stages in planning, you will have to make virtually all the suggestions and decisions for that particular stage.

Cooperative level

Classify a pupil at cooperative level for a particular stage if he or she responds as shown below:

(i) Topic: when asked to choose a topic for study, the pupil has some idea of what he or she wants to do, but you will have to help the pupil to define the topic in more specific terms.
(ii) Resources: the pupil chooses some resources, but you will need to suggest others.
(iii) Learning steps: the pupil outlines some of his or her

learning steps, but they are incomplete or need rearranging. You will need to help the pupil with the planning.

(iv) Deadlines: the pupil has a general idea how long the work will take him or her but cannot justify the time limit he or she sets.

When a pupil is at cooperative level for any one of these four stages in planning, you will have to offer suggestions and make some of the decisions. This is possibly the most common level of ability in planning.

Independent level

Classify a pupil at independent level for a particular stage if he or she responds as shown below:

(i) Topic: the pupil knows precisely what he wants to study and requires only a little, if any, prompting to be able to define a precise topic.

(ii) Resources: the pupil is able to list for himself all the resources he or she will need in order to do the work.

(iii) Learning steps: the pupil is able to outline all the necessary learning steps.

(iv) Deadlines: the pupil can estimate how long the work will take and can justify the estimate.

When a pupil is at independent level for any one of these four stages in planning, he or she is capable of providing all the ideas and making decisions for himself or herself.

Each time you assess a pupil's level of independence in planning, you note his or her level of independence for each of the four stages. For example, you may make the following assessment for the reasons given below:

Pupil: John Brown

	Level	Notes
1. Topic	Guided	He had no idea what topic he wanted to study. Suggestion was necessary.
2. Resources	Cooperative	Could suggest a few resources, but more would be needed.
3. Learning steps	Cooperative	Contributed some ideas, but additional help in organizing learning steps required.

4. Deadlines	Guided	Had no idea how long work would take him.

Note that this is an assessment for one particular independent study. On this occasion John has no idea about what he wants to do. Nor has he any idea how long the work suggested by the teacher will take him. However, once given an idea, he is able to contribute some suggestions regarding possible resources and learning steps.

On a subsequent occasion, the teacher's assessment may be different. For example, when asked to select another independent study, John might be in a position to suggest in very precise terms what he wants to do, although as on the first occasion he may require help with the other three stages.

Assessment procedure

When you first carry out an assessment of each pupil's ability to plan a piece of independent work, you may find it takes five to ten minutes to carry out the assessment procedure outlined below. However, with practice and as you become more acquainted with your pupils' ability to plan their own work, you will find it takes only a short time to make the assessment and to establish the amount of help the pupil will require. Remember that if pupils want to carry out an independent study as a pair or as a small group, you will have to assess them for their ability to plan as a pair or as a group. You will need to carry out assessments when the class is working individually on set work with which they are familiar and in the initial stages you will probably need to spread your assessment over two or three lesson periods.

Each time you assess a pupil's level of independence, it is helpful to follow a logically planned procedure. As the aim of your discussion is to find the extent to which the pupil is capable of planning the independent study without your assistance, it is important that you avoid using time during the assessment procedure to make your own suggestions. At this stage simply concentrate on making your assessment. During the assessment procedure, *for each of the four stages in planning:*
1. Ask the pupil questions of a general or specific nature as required.
2. Make judgements about the adequacy of the pupil's response.
3. Note his level of independence.

The exact procedure, with sample questions, is shown in Table 7.1. Note that the procedure follows the same pattern at each of the four stages in planning.

Table 7.1 Assessing levels of independence in planning

Stage	Procedure	Sample question
1. Defining a topic.	1. Ask a general question.	"What independent study would you like to do?
	2a. Make a quick judgement about the adequacy of the pupil's response.	
	2b. If the pupil's response to the general question was "I don't know", suggest a general topic.	"How about something to do with farming?"
	3. If necessary, ask more specific questions to help the pupil develop his ideas.	"Farming is a big topic. What particular aspect of the subject would you like to choose?"
	4. Judge the adequacy of these ideas.	
	5. If the pupil has no ideas, suggest a more specific topic.	"I know you are interested in machines. Would you like to find out what types of machines farmers use?"
2. Identifying resources	1. Ask a general question.	"What could you use in order to do your study?"
	2. Make a quick judgement about the adequacy of the pupil's response.	
	3. If necessary ask more specific questions to help the pupil develop his ideas.	"You say books and other people could help you. Have you any particular books or people in mind?"
	4. Judge the adequacy of these ideas.	
3. Outlining learning steps	1. Ask a general question.	"Tell me how you would set about doing your independent study."
	2. Make a quick judgement about the adequacy of the pupil's response.	

	3. If necessary ask more specific questions to help the pupil develop his ideas.	"Let's think about the first thing you would do in your study on Roman weapons. What would it be?"
	4. Judge the adequacy of these ideas.	
4. Setting realistic deadlines	1. Ask a general question.	"How long do you think it would take you to do this study?"
	2. Make a quick judgement about the adequacy of the pupil's response.	
	3. If necessary, ask more specific questions to help the pupil develop his ideas.	"You said you'd need three weeks to complete your study. Can you say why it will take that length of time?"
	4. Judge the adequacy of these ideas.	

Note 1. If you assess your pupil at cooperative or guided level for his or her ability to define a topic you must either help the pupil to choose a precise topic, if he or she is at the cooperative level, or supply the pupil with one, if he or she is at guided level, before continuing the discussion. This is important because unless you fix the precise area of work it will be impossible for the pupil to answer your subsequent questions relating to resources, learning steps and deadlines.

Note 2. If you have assessed a pupil at guided level for the first three stages in planning, particularly for his or her ability to outline learning steps, then it is impossible for the pupil to set a realistic deadline for his work.

Exercise 7.1

In order to assess your understanding, answer the following questions:

1. Mrs Holman asks twelve-year-old Sue to choose a topic for an independent study. Sue replies she would like to continue classwork which has already been done on the history of castles, by finding out more about the difference between Norman and medieval castles. What should Mrs Holman do next on the assessment procedure?

2. Miss Clark asks Robert, who is ten years old, what independent study he would like to do, if he had a free choice. Robert looks blank and offers no suggestion. Should Miss Clark follow this with a specific question or a suggestion?

3. Jeff is eight years old and wants to find out what sort of things float on water. The teacher asks what sort of materials he has in mind and what other resources he will need in order to carry out the study. Jeff says he will need a bowl of water and only three materials. He names cork, wood and polystyrene. What is Jeff's level of independence for the ability to identify resources?

4. Pam is in her second year at secondary school. In her social studies lesson she has chosen to do some independent work in which she plans to compare two shops in her home town, one a supermarket, the other a small, privately owned general store. She makes no response to a general question on learning steps, but suggests two steps when questioned further. What is Pam's level of independence for the ability to outline learning steps?

5. Roger is eleven years old and has chosen to examine the effects of pollution on animal life in a nearby stretch of river. His topic is an ambitious one and he cannot think how to set about his work. Should the teacher offer a suggestion?

6. Peter has not had much experience of independent work. At the end of their discussion of a piece of work which Peter will do on his own, Mr Johnson asks how long he thinks his study on the layout and content of the local newspaper will take. Peter says two weeks, which Mr Johnson thinks is reasonable. How does Mr Johnson assess Peter's level of independence?

Suggested answers to Exercise 7.1

1. Mrs Holman's next step is to ask Sue what resources she would use for her independent study. She would not ask any more questions about the topic, because Sue has defined it sufficiently precisely for Mrs Holman to assess her at independent level.

2. Miss Clark should follow her general question by suggesting a general topic to Robert. She should then follow up her suggestions with specific questions on this topic. If Robert fails to respond to the specific questions, Miss Clark should suggest a specific topic.

3. Jeff is at the cooperative level of independence for ability to identify resources. The teacher will need to suggest a greater variety of resources. For example, to make Jeff's study

worth while he will need to have available some materials which will sink, as well as those which will float.

4. Pam is at the cooperative level of independence for ability to outline learning steps. While she contributed two steps, she will need her teacher's help to organize her work fully.

5. When assessing a pupil's ability to outline learning steps, the teacher should never make any suggestions. He should follow his general question by asking specific questions to help the pupil develop his own ideas on learning steps.

6. Mr Johnson cannot assess Peter's level of independence without asking further questions which will give Peter a chance to justify the deadline he set. If Peter is then able to fully justify the deadline, he is at independent level. On the other hand, although two weeks seems a reasonable deadline, if he cannot justify it at all, he is at guided level.

Exercise 7.2

Prepare a microlesson lasting ten minutes which will give you practice in assessing one pupil's level of independence in planning. Arrange to make an audio-recording, which you can appraise afterwards.

Planning supplement

1. Your first task will be to rate your pupil's ability to define a topic for himself. However, if your pupil fails to choose a precise topic, you must be ready to suggest an appropriate subject for study, so that you are in a position to continue the assessment discussion. Think of topics which would suit the abilities and interests of the pupils concerned, so that you are prepared to offer ideas.

2. During the microlesson, remember that for each stage you should start with a general question and then follow up with more specific probing questions if these are necessary. Listed below are examples of the types of questions you can ask each pupil. Remember that the sole aim of this microlesson is to determine the pupil's levels of independence in planning four stages of the study. You are not trying to plan the work in detail at this session, so for each stage only continue your questions until you are able to make your assessment.

Defining a topic

General: 'You are going to do some work on your own. What
topic would you like to choose?'

'Tell me what independent study you would like to do.'

If necessary follow with specific questions which will help the
pupil to refine his ideas.

Specific: 'Which particular inventions would you like to find out
about?'

'What exactly would you like to study about birds?'

'What aspect of pollution are you particularly
interested in?'

If a pupil has no ideas at all, you may want to suggest a subject
area and ask him to specify a topic:

'Can you think of anything you'd like to study about
fish?'

If the pupil is still at a loss about what to suggest, you will need
to specify the precise topic for him or her:

'Well you enjoyed the recent schools' TV programmes
on "Weapons through the ages". Could you find out
more about Roman weapons?'

'You're very good at sewing, and I know you collect
dolls. Could you perhaps study the national costumes
of three countries and make costumes for the dolls?'

Identifying resources

General: 'What could you use to help with this study?'

'Where could you obtain the information you need?'

To make your questions more specific, identify a number of
particular pieces of information or materials the pupil may need.

Specific: 'Where could you find out about holidays in Greece?'

'What materials will you need to make your model
boat?'

'Where could you find water-fleas?'

Outlining learning steps

General: 'Tell me how you'd set about doing your independent
study.'

'What are all the things you'll need to do?'

If the pupil fails to respond adequately to general questions, help
him to consider the various parts of his study.

Specific: 'What will be the first job you need to do for your
study?'

'When you've read the books, have you any idea what you'll do next?'

Setting realistic deadlines

General: 'Do you know how long it will take you to do your work on the microscopic life in the pond?'
'How much time will you need to complete your study?'

If the pupil is able to answer the general question, ask him or her to explain the time estimate.

Specific: 'Why would it take that amount of time?'
'Can you explain why it would take that long?'
'How long do you think your first step would take?'

Planning guide: (Microlesson 7.2)

Answer the following and use your answers as notes to guide you in the microlesson.

1. Pupil's name: _____

2. Name three suitable topics in case the pupil has no ideas of his or her own.

   (i) _____

   (ii) _____

   (iii) _____

3(a) Prepare a general question to open the discussion on the pupil's choice of a topic.

   _____

   _____

3(b) Prepare two possible specific questions to follow up this general question.

   (i) _____

   (ii) _____

4(a) Prepare a general question you might ask to find out the pupil's ability to identify resources.

   _____

4(b) Prepare two possible specific questions to follow up this general question.

(i) _____

_____

(ii) _____

_____

5(a) Prepare a general question you might ask to find out the pupil's ability to outline learning steps.

_____

_____

5(b) Prepare two possible specific questions to follow up this general question.

(i) _____

_____

(ii) _____

_____

6(a) Prepare a general question you might ask to find out the pupil's ability to set realistic deadlines.

_____

_____

6(b) Prepare two possible specific questions to follow up this general question.

(i) _____

_____

(ii) _____

Assessment form (Microlesson 7.2)

During or immediately after your assessment discussion with the pupil, fill in the assessment form below.

Pupil's name:		
	Level	Notes
1. Topic		
2. Resources		
3. Learning steps		
4. Deadlines		

Evaluation 1 (Microlesson 7.2)

Read the appraisal guide before starting the replay of your recording.

Purpose: To give you an opportunity to check your assessment of your pupil's levels of independence in planning an independent study.

Directions: As you listen to the tape, put a tally in the appropriate

123

box in the chart below, according to your assessment of the pupil's level of independence in planning each of the four stages. Do not refer back to the assessment you have already made. Stop the tape if necessary.

Appraisal guide: Levels of independence in planning

Pupil's name		
1. Ability to define a topic	Guided level	
	Cooperative level	
	Independent level	
2. Ability to identify resources	Guided level	
	Cooperative level	
	Independent level	
3. Ability to outline learning steps	Guided level	
	Cooperative level	
	Independent level	
4. Ability to set realistic deadlines	Guided level	
	Cooperative level	
	Independent level	

Evaluation 2 (Microlesson 7.2)

Read the appraisal guide before starting the replay.

Purpose: To help you evaluate the success of your assessment procedure.

Directions: As you listen to the tape, put a tally in the appropriate box below each time you ask the pupil a general question or a specific question at each stage in the planning. Also put a tally each time you offer suggestions regarding the pupil's independent study. Remember that in some boxes you may have more than one tally.

Appraisal guide: Teacher's assessment procedure

	Teacher's contribution	Tally
1. Topic	General question	
	Specific question	
	Suggestion offered	
2. Resources	General question	
	Specific question	
	Suggestion offered	
3. Learning steps	General question	
	Specific question	
	Suggestion offered	
4. Deadlines	General question	
	Specific question	
	Suggestion offered	

Interpretation of evaluation

1. Refer to your first evaluation of the microlesson. Does your evaluation of the tape match the assessment you made during the microlesson? _____
   If they do not match, and you made an incorrect judgement when you filled in the assessment form, note down any points which will help clarify any remaining difficulties you may have in distinguishing between the three different levels of independence.

_____

_____

2. Refer to your second evaluation of the microlesson. In every instance you should have initially asked a general question.

This gives the pupil an opportunity to contribute his or her own idea. Did you ask four general questions in all, one at each stage in planning? _____

3. Compare your two evaluation forms for the microlesson.
   (a) At any stage in the planning was the pupil at the independent level? _____
   If so, did you only need to ask a general question? _____
   If you needed to follow up with a specific question only *one* should have been necessary for the pupil to respond at the independent level.
   (b) At any stage in the planning was the pupil at cooperative level? _____
   If so, check that you followed up your general question with at least two specific questions.
   (c) At any stage in the planning was the pupil at guided level? _____
   If so, check that you followed up your general question with at least two specific questions. Did the pupil answer 'I don't know' to both of these? _____

   If the pupil volunteered any information, replay the tape and check your assessment because he or she may be at the cooperative level.

4. Compare your two evaluation forms for the microlesson. The purpose of this microlesson was to assess levels of independence, not actually to plan an independent study in detail. If you had to make any suggestions for the pupil, it should only have been at the first stage in planning if the pupil was at the guided or cooperative level. Was your pupil at guided level or cooperative level for this first step in the planning? _____

   Did you specify a suitable topic for the pupil to study? _____
   Now check your second evaluation form to see if you made any suggestions for the last three stages. This should be avoided if possible.

Planning an independent study

Some time after assessing the pupil's levels of independence in planning you will need to meet the pupil to plan a complete piece of work with him or her. When the teacher and pupil meet on this occasion, their task is to discuss and agree upon the details of the study that the pupil will carry out. The intervening period between assessment and planning should have given both pupil and teacher time to give the study some additional thought.

There are seven main stages in planning, which are listed below and explained in more detail in the following subsections:

1. Stating what the pupil will learn.
2. Describing how the pupil will demonstrate what he or she has learned.
3. Identifying resources the pupil will use.
4. Specifying the pupil's learning steps.
5. Establishing checkpoints to provide feedback and monitor the pupil's progress.
6. Setting deadlines for completion of the study.
7. Arranging for an activity for the pupil to engage in immediately after the study.

The decisions made by the teacher and pupil are written down in the form of a work plan. The purpose of these work plans (pp. 148, 149) is to provide the teacher with a clear, precise statement of what is agreed with each pupil and to provide the pupil with a precise statement of what has been agreed he should do. Each of your pupils will gain more from his independent work when he participates to the fullest extent of his ability in its planning. (Figs. 7.2 and 7.3)

Fig. 7.2 Planning an independent study with one pupil.

Fig. 7.3 Planning an independent study with a pair of pupils.

1. Stating what is to be learned

In the first stage of planning, the teacher and pupil should decide on the specific knowledge or skills that the pupil is to learn. This usually involves narrowing down a broad topic such as 'history' or 'science fiction' until the initial statement is restated in terms of specific knowledge or skills. For instance, the final form of the statement for 'history' might be: 'To compare children's clothes in the early 1900s and today.' For 'science fiction' it might be: 'To compare the types of alien beings in two science fiction stories.'

It is not easy to state what is to be learned in precise terms. It is tempting to make vague statements which are open to several interpretations. An example of a precise statement is: 'To find out which are the major canals in England', whereas a vague statement would be: 'To study the English waterway system.'

Another precise statement is: 'To identify the three main weeds in the school garden.' A corresponding vague statement would be: 'To learn about weeds.'

2. Describing how learning is to be demonstrated

The second stage of planning the learning objective should also be specified precisely and be described in practical terms. It may involve writing a report, making a model, drawing a map or chart, taking a test or giving a talk to the class. The following are examples of precise practical descriptions:

1. Draw a map of the UK and mark on it five major fishing ports.
2. Construct a model of a medieval castle showing three methods of defence.
3. Give a talk to the class about the causes of the Icelandic cod 'war'.

Also, when you plan how the pupil will demonstrate what he or she has learned, an acceptable standard of performance should be agreed. This will vary considerably from one study to another. For instance, the demonstration of learning will often be in the form of a product, such as a chart. The acceptable standard of performance might be the production of a chart with five comparisons on it, with no other stipulations. On the other hand, it may be stipulated that each comparison should include at least half a page of written description and a coloured illustration. If the pupil is to take a test to demonstrate his or her learning, then the acceptable standard of performance might be to answer eight out of ten questions correctly.

3. *Identifying resources*

Probably your pupils will already be accustomed to using a number of different resources for their work in school. Books, modelling materials and pieces of equipment are resources that pupils commonly use in the classroom. Independent study gives the pupil an opportunity to choose for himself or herself the resources which he or she will need in order to carry out his independent work and also to increase the number and variety of resources the pupil can call upon and use.

When you help a pupil to identify resources, it is important that you encourage him or her to consider the wide variety of resources availabe both inside and outside the classroom.

At first it is possible that many pupils will refer only to books as their source of information. If their work in school has been book-oriented, this response is to be expected. As you develop a work plan with the pupil, try to help him or her extend his or her choice of resources. In this way the pupil can be made aware of the fact that a subject can be approached and learned in a variety of ways and that the same information can be obtained from a number of different sources.

Some independent studies lend themselves more readily than others to the use of a wide variety of resources. For example, independent work which involves a pupil in studying a subject which is observable in real life often has the advantage of calling on a whole range of resources. A pupil studying farm machinery on a nearby farm could interview the farmer, visit the farm, look at a filmstrip on farming, consult relevant books and collect any models or toys which are similar to the machines he or she is studying. Other studies which are more book-oriented may offer less scope for choice of resources. For example, a pupil may choose to study, describe and compare a number of children presented as characters in a variety of stories he or she has read recently. While this is an equally ambitious study, on this occasion choice of resources is necessarily limited to the chosen stories and discussion with others who have read the same books.

Types of resources

When you identify resources with a pupil remember that while it is useful to have a large number of resources, it is important that the pupil has experience in consulting as many different types as possible in any independent study.

1. Non-fiction books
   Types likely to be useful are:
   (a) general reference books (e.g. encyclopaedias, atlases);
   (b) textbooks (can be used as reference books, or, as in a science textbook, as a guide for conducting experiments, etc.);
   (c) books on specific subjects (e.g. 'Magnets', 'Trees').

2. Fiction books
   Types likely to be useful are:
   (a) novels based on fact (e.g. stories about animals, historical novels, stories set in particular geographical locations);
   (b) myths, legends, fairy stories;
   (c) novels, poems and plays on particular themes such as old age, poverty, town and country life.

3. Workbooks
   Programmed learning materials and workcards can also be categorized with workbooks as a particular type of reading matter. Specific exercises in a workbook or on a workcard

may relate directly to a pupil's learning objective. For example, the pupil may do a set of exercises on three- and four-sided shapes before finding examples of these shapes to be found on the school buildings. In this case the exercise serves as a measure of the extent to which the pupil has mastered a skill which is essential to the completion of his independent study.

4. Reading matter other than books
   This would include magazines, newspapers, and information pamphlets (e.g. Forestry Commission pamphlets, materials from foreign embassies and travel agencies, guides to historical buildings, etc.).

5. Audio-visual materials
   The range and number of audio-visual aids varies from one school to another. This type of resource would include any materials (e.g. TV programmes, records, slides, films, tapes, etc.) which require particular pieces of equipment (e.g. television, record-player, slide or film projector, tape-recorder) before they can be used a resources. Ideally audio-visual materials should be used to cater for individual needs in independent studies, but where this is impracticable, try at least to use them in group projects.

6. Apparatus
   This includes any equipment used for conducting experiments, such as commercially made equipment (e.g. clamp-stands, glass beakers, flasks, test-tubes, etc.) (Fig. 7.4a) as well as any domestic materials (e.g. jam jars, drinking straws, yoghurt pots) which can sometimes be used as cheap, readily available alternatives in order to carry out experiments.

7. Construction materials
   These include any man-made or natural materials a pupil may use for constructing models or displays. For example, the pupil might use wood, building blocks, straw, fabric, polystyrene foam, bottle tops, fir cones, etc.

8. Collected objects
   These include:
   (a) Any animate or inanimate objects collected by the pupil, or on the pupil's behalf, specifically for his or

her independent study. For example, for a study of grasses growing on the school playing field the pupil would collect specimens of the kinds of grasses; for a study on modern British cars the pupil might collect several toy models.

(b) Any animate or inanimate objects which are kept in the classroom by the teacher for general interest or use. For example hamsters in a cage, wall charts, photographs, models of the human eye or brain, etc.

9. Visits and outside observations

These act as useful sources of information and also provide pupils with additional motivation and interest when carrying out his or her independent work. Visits outside school (e.g. to a nature reserve, (Fig. 7.4b) historic building, museum, the seashore or a soft-drinks factory) provide opportunities for outside observations which add to the pupil's learning experience. It is possible however, for pupils to make observations without involving them in specially arranged visits. For example, a pupil could make useful observations for an independent study in the school playground, on a bus journey or walking through the town.

10. Interviews and discussions

These could be on a formal or informal basis. For example the pupil could arrange to interview a nurse and could prepare specific questions to ask her. You should encourage the pupil to think of people who could provide useful specialist information for a chosen independent study. (For example, a tradesman, shopkeeper, policeman, vicar, etc.) Parents, neighbours and school friends can also act as useful resources.

Note that the above resource list does not include the general supplies found in all classrooms. Different types of paper, paints, felt-tip pens, pencils, etc. are basic tools for independent work (Fig. 7.4c). The pupil should be made aware of the range of available materials. While it is important that you ensure that all materials are used sensibly and economically, the pupil should have ready access to them so that he or she uses them imaginatively for an independent study, without involving you unnecessarily.

Stimulatory materials

Stimulatory materials include pictures, charts, maps, living organisms, films, inanimate objects, etc. put on display in the classroom by you or your pupils. These may be carefully selected or made by you in order to arouse interest in a subject or range of subjects, or they may be made by or brought into school by pupils for the benefit of the rest of the class. Displaying a pupil's work creates interest in the classroom, and may motivate him or her to do further work, as well as acting as a stimulus to other pupils (Figs. 7.2 and 7.3).

Stimulatory materials can therefore contribute to independent study in two main ways:

1. They may be used as resources. A pupil may find amongst the materials something of relevance to his or her ongoing independent study.
2. They may act as a stimulus in providing a pupil with an idea for a new piece of work. It may be quite by chance that a pupil's interest is aroused in this way. For example, his or her attention may be caught by an aquarium containing animals from a local pond, and as a result of this the pupil may be encouraged to undertake a study on the micro-habitats of a number of water creatures.

Fig. 7.4(a) Independent studies in progress.

Fig. 7.4(b) Independent studies in progress.

Fig. 7.4(c) Independent studies in progress.

Stimulatory materials may also be used by you deliberately to draw your pupils' attention to a particular topic and to structure their choice of independent work. These materials may take the form of prepared charts, an organized class visit or a talk by an outside speaker. By providing these stimulatory materials, you will create interest in the subject, and you can then build on this interest in future independent work. This may take the form of a large-scale study in which individuals or small groups carry out independent work which contributes to the complete study. For example in a class project on 'Our Village', choices of independent work could range from a study of the village shopping facilities to an illustrated account of the local architecture.

Availability of resources

When you identify resources with a pupil for his or her chosen independent study it is important that you both bear in mind the availability of the pupil's chosen resources. Make sure that the pupil is in a position to have access to them, and that he or she knows how to set about acquiring and using them. It may be necessary for you or some other person to help the pupil write a letter, organize a visit or an interview, but remember that activities such as these and the acquisition of other resources all contribute to the pupil's experience of independent work.

Different schools organize their own resources in a variety of ways. Your pupils may be accustomed to using a resource area which is available for the use of all pupils in the school. However, if you work in an enclosed classroom situation or if a central resource area does not exist in your school, you may find it helpful to prepare a list of resources for your own class. A card index indicating the whereabouts of a particular resource is an efficient mechanism for developing such a list. Pupils could consult this either for ideas or to help them locate their required resource in the classroom.

Discussing resources with a pupil

While you can refer all the class to a catalogue of resources, when you discuss a work plan with an individual pupil it is important to try and help the pupil choose the resources which are most appropriate in order to achieve the learning objectives. Once you have established a pupil's level of independence and have discussed several work plans with him or her you will be familiar with the types of resources which are most helpful to that pupil when carrying out independent work. Remember that resources motivate the pupil to learn. It would be unhelpful, for example, if a poor reader were referred to a number of books as his or her only resource.

4. Specifying learning steps

Learning steps are the tasks a pupil undertakes in order to complete his or her independent study. These should be arranged in logical sequence. For example a pupil may decide to do an independent study which demands that he or she find out where the children in his class live in relation to the school and how they travel to and from school each day. The pupil will show what he or she has learned by mounting a display for the rest of the class and writing a short account of his or her conclusions. The pupil's learning steps can be listed in the following way:

1. Find out from all children in the class where they live and how they travel to and from school.
2. Prepare a large-scale street map of the area to be covered.
3. Mark on the map where children live, using symbols showing how they travel to and from school.
4. Make a chart showing different means of travel. Indicate the total number of children cycling, walking, etc.
5. Write a brief account of conclusions.
6. Mount map, chart and written conclusions for display in classroom.

Remember that there may be any number of learning steps, depending on the nature and size of the study. It is possible that you may want to divide one step into a number of shorter, simpler steps. In this way less able or less independent pupils will be faced with smaller, more manageable tasks. For instance, steps 1 and 2 above could be described in more detail as follows if this would help the pupil set about the work more confidently and more efficiently:

1(a) Divide a piece of paper into three columns.
1(b) Head the columns: name, address, means of travel.
1(c) Obtain the information from each child in the class and write it down.

2(a) Borrow street map of the area from the teacher.
2(b) Decide on the area to be covered and the number of times it has to be enlarged.

2(c) Obtain necessary drawing materials.

2(d) Draw large-scale street map.

When you discuss learning steps with your pupil, make sure you take into account the following points:

1. All the necessary steps for achieving the learning objectives should be included. Failure to note down a step might lead to confusion on the part of the pupil, or the pupil might fail to complete an essential part of his or her work.
2. The learning steps must be organized logically. In this way you will be training the pupil to work systematically towards the achievement of his or her learning objectives.
3. The pupil should be involved in a variety of activities. Try and encourage your pupils to engage in activities other than reading and writing. New or unusual activities will encourage the pupil to become more lively and imaginative in his or her approach to independent work and a variety of activities will also widen the pupil's learning experience.

5. *Establishing checkpoints*

The next stage in the work plan is to decide when the pupil will need feedback on his or her progress. This stage is referred to as 'establishing checkpoints'. As well as providing positive reinforcement when the pupil's progress is satisfactory, this system alerts both teacher and pupil to any problems and allows remedial action to be taken.

You should consider the provision of some type of feedback, at least at the end of each learning step. It may also be necessary to provide feedback during a long learning step. For example, if one learning step in a study on crystals was 'grow crystals of copper sulphate', it would probably be helpful for the pupil to receive feedback while he or she is setting up the experiment.

It will be necessary to bear in mind the pupil's ability and the nature of the work when you both discuss the points at which checkpoints will be necessary and what methods will be appropriate.

Making feedback effective

If feedback is to be effective in maintaining the pupil's motivation it must satisfy certain criteria. In order to satisfy these criteria in a busy classroom, a variety of feedback methods should be used. The pupil should check his or her work with you only if it is considered to be essential. Feedback is appropriate only if it satisfies the following criteria:

Feedback should tell the pupil what he needs to know, i.e. provide relevant information.

Feedback should be provided when it is needed.

Feedback should involve the minimum necessary use of the teacher.

The following feedback techniques can give the pupil rapid and accurate information on his progress:

1. *Use of reference materials.* Very often, information obtained by the pupil can be cross-checked against other reference materials. Also, a finished product such as a map, chart or model can be checked against the original reference materials.
2. *Consultation with other pupils.* If several pupils are working in the same general subject or topic area they can often check their work with each other. This may take the form of a discussion between two pupils or a small group discussion, which may be initiated by the teacher.
3. *Tests.* As part of an independent study, a pupil may need to learn specific facts or skills. A short test could provide appropriate feedback. Answer sheets place more responsibility on the pupil as he or she is expected to mark his or her own tests.
4. *Consultation with adults other than teacher.* It may sometimes be appropriate for feedback to come from another adult. For example, the school librarian may check a pupil's choice of books. Parents may also provide useful feedback, e.g. checking letters, etc.
5. *Pupil ticks completed activities.* Some learning steps are such that the pupil does not need to check the accuracy of his or her work, e.g. reading a particular book. For this type of activity, the checkpoint may involve only ticking the work plan to show that the step has been completed.
6. *Consultation with the teacher.* Checkpoints should involve pupil–teacher interaction only at the most critical points in the independent study or when other methods are not available or appropriate. Checking with the teacher is generally appropriate when the pupil has completed his work. At other times the ability of the pupil and the nature of his work must be considered. Teacher–pupil interaction reminds the pupil that the teacher is interested in his or her work.

6. Setting deadlines

When planning an independent study, setting deadlines serves two useful purposes; it trains the pupil to work to specific time limits and it keeps the teacher in touch with the pupil's progress.

To be effective, deadlines must be suited to the work rate of the individual pupil. At first it may be difficult to set realistic deadlines. You may find that a pupil finishes his or her work before the prearranged deadline and has time to spare. On the other hand, the pupil may fail to meet the deadline because he or she cannot work as quickly as anticipated. In either case you will have gained valuable information on the speed at which the pupil can work. This will help you to set more realistic deadlines for the next independent study.

It is also possible that a pupil may fail to meet a deadline because he or she is having unexpected difficulty with the work. In this case you will be alerted to the need for assistance. It is appropriate to set more frequent deadlines for less able pupils. The deadlines should be based on the learning steps in the work plan. Even when it is not necessary to set a deadline for each learning step, the estimate of the time required for the complete study should be based on every learning task the pupil will undertake. When deciding how many intermediate deadlines to set, both the size of the individual learning tasks and the ability of the pupil to work independently should be considered.

For example, Peter is eleven years old and is in his final year at junior school. He is a responsible child of average ability. In his independent study he will find out about traffic noise outside his school. For each of his learning steps listed below, the decision whether or not to set a deadline is noted.

Learning Steps	Deadlines	Reasons
1. Obtain book on noise from library and read chapter on measuring noise levels.	Yes	To help Peter regulate his work and meet deadline for step 4.
2. Borrow noise-level meter from Mr Smith at local secondary school.	No	Peter can see Mr Smith any lunchtime.
3. Prepare table for recording noise levels.	No	Simple, short task.
4. Measure noise levels outside school.	Yes	End of experimental stage of work.

5. Make chart showing noise levels made by vehicles.	No	Closely related to step 6.
6. Prepare talk for class.	Yes	Final deadline always required.

Setting deadlines for the learning steps shown leaves Peter to make sure that he completes steps 2 and 3 in time to meet his deadline for step 4. He also has to time his work for step 5 for himself. Some pupils may require fewer deadlines. On the other hand, some may require a deadline for every learning step.

7. Post-project activity

When all your pupils are engaged in independent study, it is unlikely that you will be available to see a particular pupil immediately he or she has finished the work. It is suggested that as the seventh and last stage in planning the study, you should arrange an activity for the pupil to carry out when he or she has finished the study. This is an important management tool as the pupil will know what to do while he or she is waiting to see you.

This post-project activity should involve a change in activity after the independent study and should preferably be something the pupil wants to do. Examples of suitable activities are: continuing to read a particular book, making a model, painting, pottery, feeding animals kept in the classroom, planting bulbs or seeds. Many other possible activities will probably come to mind.

The rationale behind the use of a detailed work plan for each pupil's independent study is that all the pupils in the class know what they should be doing throughout their independent studies and can work effectively without constant supervision by the teacher. The following points may help you to ensure that independent studies operate efficiently. A programme of independent study can be unsuccessful because pupils demand unnecessary assistance from the teacher in solving routine problems which arise when they are working independently. This diverts the teacher's attention from such significant tasks as developing work plans, discussing a pupil's progress or bringing a number of pupils together to share the new skills and knowledge they have acquired.

Individual problems are bound to arise and pupils should be encouraged from the start to try and solve them on their own. However, confusion and uncertainty can be prevented if you take time to carry out discussions with the pupils on the following lines:

1. Alert the pupils to possible practical or routine difficulties which they will all experience and which can be dealt with immediately. One type of problem a pupil may meet concerns the difficulty of finding or using certain materials in the classroom. For example, problems occur when a pupil needs a particular piece of equipment or book and cannot find it in the agreed place. Make a named pupil responsible for a particular set of books, equipment, etc. and stress the importance of keeping materials in the place assigned to them.

2. Make the pupils aware of the times when they can appropriately discuss any problems with you, i.e.
(a) When developing their work plan.
   When developing the work plan it is important for the teacher to clarify any points which bother the pupil at this stage. You should also be on the alert for possible problems which might arise at later stages in the work.
(b) At checkpoints.
   An established checkpoint with you is an ideal time for the pupil to discuss any other problems which have arisen or which the pupil foresees in the next learning steps.

3. But however careful the planning, some unforseen problems are bound to arise during a pupil's work. If the pupil cannot get help from other pupils, he or she will need to consult you. For instance there are occasions when you might need to revise a pupil's entire work plan during an independent study. If a pupil fails to meet the deadlines it is possible that the deadlines set were not realistic in terms of the pupil's ability. Revision of the deadlines may be necessary. It is possible that the study is too difficult for the pupil or that the learning steps are too involved and need to be stated in more detail. If you notice that the pupil is wasting time there are two possible explanations. The learning steps may be too involved and need revision or possibly the work is not challenging enough for the pupil.

There may be occasions when you will want to allow pupils, particularly those of higher ability, more flexibility in their work. This can be accomplished by modifying the learning objectives in line with the pupil's new ideas. Any change in the objectives will also require changes in the later stages of the work plan.

Exercise 7.3

1. Prepare a microlesson lasting twenty minutes which will give you practice in helping a pupil to plan all the stages of an independent study.
2. Choose a pupil for whom you have already assessed level of independence in planning. Arrange for your discussion to be recorded either on audiotape or videotape.
3. Encourage as much participation in the planning from the pupil at every stage.
4. The dialogue below shows the course that a planning session might take. John is in his second year at a secondary school.

Teacher: Yesterday, you decided that you would like to do some independent work on steel, John. Have you thought of any more ideas?

John: I could find out how steel is made.

Teacher: What exactly would you hope to find out about steel-making?

John: What do you mean?

Teacher: Well, what aspects of steel manufacture would you like to look into?

John: I know that steel comes from iron ore, I would start by learning about iron ore, where it comes from and what is done to it. Then I would find out how the iron ore is turned into steel and what steel is used for.

Teacher: When you have found all this out, how could you show me, and the rest of the class, that you have learned how steel is made?

John: You could give me a test.

Teacher: But it would only show me what you know. Can you think of a better way, that would show the rest of the class?

John: I could make a chart.

Teacher: What would you show on the chart?

John: I think I could show where iron ore comes from, how it is turned into steel and how the steel is made into different things.

Teacher: Good. But you won't have time to discover all the uses of steel. How many do you think you will be able to find?

John: How about five?

Teacher: That's good. Now, how would you find all this information?

John: I could go to the library.

Teacher: What sort of books would you use?

John: I read about steel in *Understanding Science*. I could look at the encyclopaedias and chemistry books as well.

Teacher: Very good. Is there anywhere else from which you could get some information?

John: I don't know.

Teacher: Well, who makes steel?

John: The British Steel Corporation.

Teacher: Very good. Could you get some information from them?

John: I'm not sure. I would have to write to them and ask for help.

Teacher: I think we have a filmstrip on steel-making. Would you like to look at it?

John: Yes.

Teacher: Well now, can you tell me everything you will need? to do?

John: I'll need to write to the British Steel Corporation first, because they will take some time to reply. While I'm waiting, I'll look at the film and go to the library and find out about steel in the encyclopaedia, the chemistry books and *Understanding Science*. By then the material from the British Steel Corporation should have arrived and I can look at that before I make the chart.

Teacher: Will you need to check what you are doing at any stage?

John: Perhaps I should check the letter to see if it is all right.

Teacher: Who would you check it with?

John: My father.

Teacher: That's a good idea. What next?

John: I should check the books I use. The librarian should be able to help me.

Teacher: Very good. What will you need to check next?

John: When I've found out all about the way steel is made, I should check before I start the chart.

Teacher: How would you do this?

John: I think I should come and see you.

Teacher: All right. Now we come to the awkward part. How long is all this going to take? Remember you will have one hour a week at school, and homework time, for

143

	doing this work.
John:	About a month.
Teacher:	Well, let's look at each part of your work. How long will it take to write the letter?
John:	I can do that today.
Teacher:	Right. How long to watch the film and do the reading?
John:	Probably about two weeks if I go to the library during science lessons and at lunch times.
Teacher:	If you get a quick reply to your letter, how long do you think you will need to study the information they send?
John:	Would a week do?
Teacher:	Probably, depending on the amount of material they send you. How long will it take you to make the chart?
John:	I'd like to work on it at home. I think perhaps one week to plan it and one week to make it.
Teacher:	So how long is that altogether?
John:	Five weeks.
Teacher:	Your estimate was very good. When you have finished the chart and checked it with me, what would you like to do?
John:	I'd like to make some model animals out of glass.
Teacher:	Can you manage that?
John:	I think so. Mr Johnson let me do some glass-blowing last year and I would like to do some more.
Teacher:	All right, but I want you to check with Mr Brown our technician, to make sure that you have all the right equipment. Now, let's make sure we have all this written down so we both know exactly what you are going to do.

Work plan – pupil's copy

Pupil: _____John Ward_____

Teacher: _____Mr Smith_____   Date: ___3 February, 1975___

What will you learn?	How will you show what you have learned?
1. Where iron ore comes from	Construct a chart showing all the

2. How iron ore is processed	things listed
3. How iron ore is turned into steel	
4. Five uses of steel	

What resources will you use? Encyclopaedia, chemistry books, 'Understanding Science', filmstrip on steel-making, British Steel Corporation literature.

Learning steps	Checkpoints	Deadlines
1. Write to British Steel Corporation	Check with father	3 February
2. Look at filmstrip		
3. Read books, magazine and BSC literature	Check with librarian	24 February
4. Plan chart	Check with teacher	3 March
5. Make chart	Show to teacher and hang on wall for class to see	10 March

Date for finishing work: 10 March

What will you do when you have finished? Glass-blowing

Planning guide (Microlesson 7.3)

Answer the following and use your answers as notes to guide you in the microlesson. Also work plans are provided for your use on pp. 148 and 149.

1. Pupil's name: _____
2. Levels of independence in planning:

   Topic: _____ Resources: _____

   Learning Steps:_____ Deadlines: _____

3. Write down the seven stages in planning and any notes
necessary for each stage.

Stage 1:_____

_____

_____

_____

_____

Stage 2:_____

_____

_____

_____

_____

Stage 3:_____

_____

_____

_____

_____

Stage 4:_____

_____

_____

_____

_____

_____

Stage 5: _____

_____

_____

_____

_____

Stage 6: _____

_____

_____

_____

_____

Stage 7: _____

_____

_____

_____

_____

_____

Work plan – Teacher's copy

Pupil: _____

Teacher: _____   Date: _____

What will you learn?	How will you show what you have learned?

What resources will you use? _____

_____

_____

Learning steps	Checkpoints	Deadlines

Date for finishing work: _____

What will you do when you have finished? _____

_____

Work plan – Pupil's copy

Pupil: _____

Teacher: _____ Date: _____

What will you learn?	How will you show what you have learned?

What resources will you use? _____

_____

_____

Learning steps	Checkpoints	Deadlines

Date for finishing work: _____

What will you do when you have finished? _____

_____

Evaluation 1 (Microlesson 7.3: First replay)

Read the appraisal guide before starting the replay.

Purpose: To help you evaluate your performance at each of the seven stages involved in the development of a work plan.

Directions: Play the whole tape, stopping it when necessary.

   As you listen to the microlesson, rate each of the seven stages in planning by placing a tally in the appropriate boxes in the guide below.

Appraisal Guide: Stages in Planning

Stage 1: Stating what is to be learned

Stated in precise terms	Stated in general terms terms	Only stated briefly

Stage 2: Describing how learning will be demonstrated

Described in vague terms	Acceptable standard of performance not finalized	Described in precise terms

Stage 3: Identifying available resources

Type of resource	Tick if used
Non-fiction books	
Fiction books	
Workbooks	
Reading matter other than books	
Audio-visual materials	
Apparatus	

Construction materials	
Collected objects	
Visits and outside observations	
Interviews and discussions	

Stage 4: Specifying learning steps

Learning step	Logical sequence	Illogical sequence	Too much detail	Too little detail	Appropriate detail
1					
2					
3					
4					
5					
6					
7					
8					
9					
10					

Stage 5: Establishing checkpoints

	Checkpoint					
	1	2	3	4	5	6
Does the feedback provide relevant information?						
Is the feedback provided as soon as it is needed?						
Does the feedback involve the minimum use of the teacher?						

Is the feedback appropriate?	

Stage 6: Setting deadlines

Overall deadline not based on learning steps	Overall deadline based on learning steps

Stage 7: Arranging a post-project activity

Post-project activity not arranged	Post-project activity arranged

Evaluation 2 (Microlesson 7.3: Second replay)

Read the appraisal guide before starting the replay.

Purpose: To help you evaluate your interaction with the pupil while planning the independent study.

Directions: Play the whole tape, stopping it when necessary.

For each decision made during the planning (e.g. one resource or one checkpoint) place a tick in the appropriate box in the guide below. You may well have more than one tick in a box.

Appraisal Guide: Teacher–pupil interaction

	Teacher suggests without questioning pupil	Teacher invites pupil suggestion	Pupil volunteers suggestion
1. Stating what is to be learned			
2. Describing how learning will be demonstrated			
3. Identifying available resources			

4. Specifying learning steps			
5. Establishing checkpoints			
6. Setting deadlines			
7. Arranging a post-project activity			

Interpretation of Microlesson 7.3

1. Refer to your evaluation form for Stages 1 and 2, first replay: Are the learning objectives precise? _____
   Refer to your evaluation form for Stages 1 and 2, the second replay. Are you inviting suggestion from the pupil as much as possible? _____
   How can you improve your planning of learning objectives?

   _____

   _____

   _____

   _____

2. Refer to your evaluation of your first replay for Stage 3: Were a variety of resources identified? _____
   Refer to your evaluation of your second replay for Stage 3: Are you inviting suggestions from the pupil as much as possible? _____
   How can you improve your planning of resources?

   _____

   _____

   _____

   _____

3. Refer to your evaluation for your first and second replays for Stage 4:
   How can you improve your planning of learning steps?

   _____

   _____

   _____

   _____

4. Refer to your evaluation of your first and second replays for Stage 5:
   How can you improve your planning of checkpoints?

   _____

   _____

   _____

   _____

5. Refer to your evaluation of your first and second replays for Stage 6:
   How can you improve your planning of deadlines?

   _____

   _____

   _____

   _____

6. Refer to your evaluation of your first and second replays for Stage 7:
   Was a post-project activity arranged? _____
   If so, was the activity chosen by the pupil? _____

Introducing independent studies to a new class

When you start independent studies with pupils who are not used to working in this way you will find it useful to follow a carefully planned procedure. A number of activities are listed below which will help you to introduce independent studies to a new class.

Discuss pupils' previous experience of working independently

If you are a secondary school teacher and at the beginning of the school year you decide to start independent studies with a first-year class, you are dealing with pupils who are not only new to you but who also have had different experiences of working on their own. Some pupils may have experienced only a formal classroom situation, some may have a limited experience of working on their own, while others may come from entirely informal classrooms.

It is important to know what previous experience your pupils have of independent work and you should make a point of discussing this with them. If you teach in a junior school most of them will have had the same amount of experience of working on their own. There are three main types of information you should try to find out:

(a) Have they ever worked on their own or in small groups?
(b) What sort of work have they done on their own?
(c) Did they enjoy working on their own or in small groups?

Describe what you mean by 'independent studies' and how it will function in your classroom.

Having held the discussion you are in a position to know more precisely how your pupils are going to react to independent work. Keeping their comments in mind, prepare a list of points which will help you describe independent studies to them. Tell the class in clear, simple terms what independent studies will involve.

Explain that:

(a) They will sometimes work on their own and sometimes in pairs or small groups.
(b) Before any pupil starts a piece of independent work, he will meet with you to plan it in detail.
(c) You will be doing this so that each pupil will know precisely what he has to do for each study.
(d) By doing this the pupil will be better prepared to work on his own without having to consult you or any other person unnecessarily.

(e) You expect each pupil to be responsible for his own work.

Reassure your pupils, however, that you will be following their progress with interest, and that you will know exactly what each pupil is doing because you will have planned the work together beforehand.

Also tell the class what to expect of you. Explain that you are there to guide them in the planning of their work, although you would like each pupil to have his own ideas about his work and how he will carry it out. Point out to the pupils that you may sometimes need to check the progress of their work and that you will be keen to see it, whatever form it should take, when it is completed. Decide what you will tell the class about your role during independent study times. For example, if you think it best to move freely about the classroom for the entire study period, tell the class you will be doing this. However, just describe your role in general terms for the time being, as you will want to establish a procedure whereby a pupil can consult you during independent studies, when you discuss the work plan in more detail.

You should make clear to the pupils what standard of behaviour you expect, regarding talking and movement within the classroom. Also inform pupils of the extent to which they are free to go to other parts of the school, such as the library.

Discuss the work plan and each of its stages

Once you have described independent studies in general terms and have indicated what this means for both you and the pupils, talk more specifically about the work plan itself.

Begin by telling the pupils how the work plan fits into the overall framework for independent studies. Make the following points:

(a) You will begin by meeting each pupil or group of pupils in turn to talk very briefly about the work. (This will allow you to carry out your assessment procedure.)

(b) One or two days later, when you have both had more time to think about the chosen work, you will meet again to discuss it in much more detail. Together you will draw up a work plan.

Spend some time going through the work plan in detail. Before you define each stage for them, ask the pupils to think of a number of topics and then choose one of their contributions which has a general appeal and which you can use as a sample topic for an independent study. Then go through each stage of the work plan, describing it carefully and simply, introducing the pupils to terms which may be new to them, such as checkpoints and deadlines, and illustrating each stage using the chosen topic. In this way you will build up a sample work plan. Write this up on the board or on a large sheet of paper which can be displayed in the classroom. You may also like each pupil to enter the details of the sample independent study on a copy of the work plan. This will acquaint each of them with the idea of having a personal work plan which the pupil completes for himself or herself and which is a written reminder of every stage of the independent study and what it will involve.

When you discuss resources with your pupils, show them where resources are kept in the classroom. Inform them which can be obtained freely at any time. If you think it necessary, establish the procedure for obtaining other resources such as pieces of equipment. You might also like to make certain pupils in the class responsible for looking after and distributing particular materials. However, make sure that your pupils do not limit their idea of resources to what is in the classroom. Ask them to list other resources in the school, their homes, the community.

If you plan to use a card index system which indicates the whereabouts of a particular resource, explain how it might be used and how pupils might add to it after completing an independent study.

When the pupils collect resources, carry out learning steps and check their work with you or any other pupil or teacher, they will be involved in movement around the classroom and/or school. Depending on your own school situation you will need to decide for yourself the extent to which you are able to allow freedom of movement. While, on the one hand, you want the pupils to go about their work independently and responsibly without involving you unnecessarily, the amount of noise and movement must be controlled if the classroom is to maintain an atmosphere which is conducive to work.

There will be occasions when pupils need to consult you: at prearranged checkpoints, at the end of a study and whenever unexpected problems arise. If you find it difficult to establish any general ruling about what a pupil should do in these situations, at least make it clear that pupils should not interrupt when they see you discussing work with another pupil. Also, they should avoid congregating round you in large groups waiting for you to attend to them. While waiting they should engage in their post-project activities until it is convenient for you to see them.

Remember that many of the management problems in your classroom will be reduced:

(a) If your assessment of each pupil's levels of independence has been carried out carefully and if the subsequent planning has been done on the basis of this assessment.

(b) If you use your copy of each pupil's work plan as a guide to what he or she should be doing at any particular time.

You may need to discuss suitable post-project activities with your class and explain the purpose they serve in independent studies. Discuss the types of activities which could be employed, and if you feel it would be helpful, draw up a list of suitable activities suggested by the pupils. Make it clear that the choice of activity will be subject to your approval and will depend to some extent on practical restrictions in the classroom, such as available space, the noise involved, etc. Be sure that the pupils understand that post-project activities should in no way interfere with the work of other pupils.

Assess levels of independence in planning

Having discussed the work plan with your pupils, your next task will be to assess their levels of independence in planning. You may feel it would be easier if pupils worked on their own for their first independent study. However, if you feel it would give them more confidence to tackle the work in pairs or groups, then give them this choice.

Before you start assessing levels of independence, assign set work with which the pupils are familiar to the class so that each pupil works on his own. By doing this you will have the class usefully employed while you make your assessment of individuals or small groups.

Once your pupils are working on their own, you are then in a position to talk with individual pupils or small groups in order to assess their levels of independence. Remember that at this stage you are not planning any work in detail, but merely establishing a topic with each pupil or group and finding out the amount of help you will need to contribute to the planning in each case.

Plan independent studies in detail

Once you have assessed all the pupils for their levels of

independence in planning, you can start to develop complete work plans with individuals or small groups. While you do this, the class can continue working on their individual assignments as outlined above. It is not necessary for the entire class to begin independent studies at the same time. But make sure that the pupils who start their independent studies first do not finish their work before you complete the planning with the rest of the pupils. To do this, you will need to estimate the total planning time. In this way it can be ensured that the rest of your planning sessions will not be interrupted by pupils who have completed their studies. It might be useful if the pupils who start their independent studies first are those you think are likely to settle down quickly and happily to working in this way.

A schedule of activities for your use when introducing independent studies to a new class is given below.

Schedule of activities for introducing independent studies to a new class

This schedule is intended to be of use to you when introducing a new class to independent studies. The schedule is not intended to be binding in any way, but it gives you the opportunity to plan ahead and actually fix dates and times for each of the activities. The length of time each activity is likely to take is suggested, based on a class size of thirty. These times are approximate, however, and can be altered to suit your own circumstances. For example, the time taken to assess pupils' levels of independence in planning and to develop work plans with them will depend on various factors such as the number of pupils in your class and their ability to plan independent work. As these discussions with individuals must be carried out when the class is busy with individual work, it will probably take approximately a week to accomplish all these tasks.

Date and time

1. Discussion on pupils' previous experience of working independently. (Half an hour) _____

2. Discussion with class on what is meant by independent studies. (One hour) _____

3. Discussion on the work plan and development of a sample plan. (Three hours) _____

4. Assessing pupils' levels of independence in planning while organized classwork is in progress. (Three hours) _____

5. Developing work plans with pupils
   (Eight hours)

Planning for studies outside the school

Studies outside the school present the teacher with a situation in which easy contact with each pupil is not possible. (Fig. 7.5) Therefore, independent or small-group work, to which the techniques already described can be applied, is the usual solution. But, it is important to remember that there are also some differences between classroom studies and those which take place outside the school.

Fig. 7.5   Classwork out of doors.

The time allocation made to studies outside the school usually needs to be precise owing to the other commitments of both teacher and pupils. Therefore, careful preliminary study of the site and careful timing of the required fieldwork, made in advance by the teacher, is essential to efficient planning of this type of work.

Frequently fieldwork involves collecting data which is required for follow-up work in the classroom. In such a case the time allocated to this part of a study must be related to the time remaining for the follow up which will enable the data to be usefully applied. (Figs. 7.6a and 7.6b)

Fig. 7.6(a) Follow-up work in the classroom.

Fig. 7.6(b) Follow-up work in the classroom.

Even if the entire class is working as a single group in the field, careful advance planning is necessary, so that pupils are absolutely clear about the work to be undertaken, without further explanation. For example, if it is intended that the whole class shall follow a nature trail, it is essential that a leaflet or guide is prepared which draws attention to the special features or situations to be observed and recorded. (Fig. 7.7) Because the

Fig. 7.7   Studying the nature trail guide.

Fig. 7.8   Answering questions posed by the nature trail guide.

supervision of all pupils in such a situation is not feasible, it is important that the teacher devises a guide which encourages the pupil to learn through his own efforts. This can be achieved by devising a guide which uses a questioning, rather than a descriptive, approach (Fig. 7.8) and by allowing sufficient time after the fieldwork is over for a class discussion on their observations.

Example: A portion of a nature trail guide to a woodland
Point 4
Yew (*Taxus baccata*)
You are standing under a yew tree. Study the ground and compare it with the ground under the other trees near by.

(a) Look at the soil and notice the absence of plants. Give three reasons which could explain why plants do not grow on the soil under yew trees?

(i) _____

(ii) _____

(iii) _____
Now look at the ground near the stump that has been left behind when a yew tree was cut down and removed.

(b) Do you notice any difference between this area and the area under the yew tree?

_____

(c) What conditions will have changed as a result of the removal of the yew tree?

_____

(d) What characteristics of mosses make them particularly suited to pioneering the colonization of this bare ground?

_____

(e) What further changes would be necessary before flowering plants are able to succeed the mosses?

_____

Small-group investigations made out of doors are also frequently arranged by teachers. In such cases resources such as maps, equipment, books, etc. have to be taken to the site. (Fig. 7.9) This again requires very careful planning on the part of the teacher with regard to the feasibility of the investigation planned, the time required to carry it out and the equipment to be taken into the field and the type of follow-up work to be carried out in the classroom.

Fig. 7.9   Small group work out of doors – taking the equipment to the site.

Apart from the planning which the teacher carries out with individuals and small groups, outdoor work with a class usually involves a short preliminary discussion with the class as a whole, on (1) codes of conduct, e.g. observation of the Countryside Code, (2) timing, (3) work to be carried through, (4) footwear and suitable clothing. It is essential that all pupils are clear on all these points. Likewise, it is essential that time is allocated following a field visit for (1) return of resources, e.g. equipment, books, etc., (2) dealing with data collected and (3) a class discussion which can provide valuable feedback for the teacher.

Sample work plans involving both field and classroom studies.
Work plan

Pupil: Sheila Gregson (10 years)

Teacher: Mr Whittaker   Date: Monday 1 July

What will you learn?	How will you show what you have learned?
1. The intensity of noises produced by common sources, e.g. car at a distance of 10 m in a restricted zone.	1. Construction of data sheet with intensity and description of noise.
2. Location of noise sources in residential and industrial areas of Lancaster.	2(a) Display a map of Lancaster showing location of noise sources.
	(b) Prepare a report for class.

What resources will you use?   Tape-recorder, tape of various

noises to accompany data sheet of intensity of noises. Street map of

Lancaster. Drawing pins of different colours. Drawing materials.

Learning steps	Checkpoints	Deadlines
1. Collect map, data sheet and tape-recorder. Listen to tape.	Check with technician	Mon. 1 July
2. Visit a number of industrial and residential areas of Lancaster and listen for sounds coming from factories, buses, etc. Tape them.		Wed. 3 July
3. Using data sheet provided so that comparisons can be made, compile your own data sheet showing intensity and description of 'your' noise sources.		Fri. 5 July
4. Pin up the map of Lancaster on the noise board and indicate the different noise sources and their intensities.		Mon. 8 July
5. Prepare report to class.	Submit work to teacher and arrange a time to give a report to class	Wed. 10 July

Date for finishing work: 10 July.

What will you do when you have finished?   Mount and identify plants for joint study on weeds in school garden.

Work plan

Pupil: Angela Burns (11 years)

Teacher: Miss Severn   Date: Monday 1 March

What will you learn?	How will you show what you have learned?
1. Identification of six species of freshwater animal 2. Methods of movement shown by the six animals	1. Presentation of names on chart to class 2(a) Presentation of a report to the class on detailed observations of movement. (b) Presentation of a chart showing the differences in the methods of movement (e.g. crawling, swimming without legs, etc.)

What resources will you use?   Books, filmstrip on pond animals,

chart, paintbrush, white tray, lens, aquarium containing

water-boatmen, leeches, flatworms, shrimps, snails, caddis-fly

larvae.

Learning steps	Checkpoints	Deadlines
1. Collect books and equipment	Check with librarian	Mon. 1 March
2. Select six different animal types and identify them using a key or books	Check using filmstrip with notes	Mon. 1 March
3. Observe each animal individually and note how it moves		Mon. 8 March
4. Prepare chart and report for class	Submit work to teacher and arrange time for giving report to class	Wed. 10 March

Date for finishing work: 10 March.

What will you do when you have finished?   Painting eggs for

Easter competition at school.

Work plan

Pupil: Barbara Davis (10 years)

Teacher: Mr Hurst   Date: Monday 8 March

What will you learn?	How will you show what you have learned?
History of local church from 1850 to present day with particular reference to architectural features	File containing written and illustrated account

What resources will you use?   Vicar and/or churchwarden,

library book on history of village. File, drawing materials, etc.

Camera.

Learning steps	Checkpoints	Deadlines
1. Obtain and read books on village history	Local librarian	Fri. 12 March
2. Visit church, take photographs, draw sketches	Discuss points of interest with vicar/warden	Sat. 20 March
3. See vicar/warden. Consult literature on church, also archives if appropriate	Tick on list	Sat. 20 March
4. Write chronological list of architectural changes	Vicar/warden	Sat. 27 March
5. Prepare illustrations for file	Art teacher	Thur. 1 April
6. Write account and present in file	Teacher	Mon. 5 April

What will you do when you have finished? Write poems for
school magazine.

Work plan

Pupil: Michael Jolley (13 years)

Teacher: Mr Holmes   Date: Monday 7 January

What will you learn?	How will you show what you have learned?
1. Measurement of growth of twig length by means of girdle scars and growth in thickness by counting annual rings 2. Comparison of the growth rates of five different types of trees	1. Presentation of report to class using a log with important dates marked in the annual rings 2. Presentation of data tables and a number of logs of similar thickness with age indicated

What resources will you use? Books, lens, filmstrip describing

and explaining annual rings. Forestry Commission (for

information on growth rates). Logs, magnifying glasses, pins,

scissors, sticky paper. Access to at least five different types of tree,

the names of which are known.

Learning steps	Checkpoints	Deadlines
1. Write to Forestry Commission for details on growth rates, particularly of the types of trees being studied	Check with older brother	Mon. 7 Jan.
2. Collect books from library	Check with librarian	Mon. 7 Jan.
3. Look for scars on twigs and find out, using books, what caused them		
4. Find out if the five trees show differences in the rate at which their length	Check with information from Forestry Commission	Mon. 14 Jan.

increases. Make data tables for class		
5. Collect filmstrip and study 'annual rings'	Check with technician	Wed. 16 Jan.
6. Calculate the ages of trees when felled by examining annual rings. Pin flags in one log only, at important dates supplied by classmates (e.g. England won the World Cup in 1966)	Submit work to teacher and arrange a time when report will be given to the class	Fri. 18 Jan.

Date for finishing work: 18 January

What will you do when you have finished?   Continuation of

investigation into the differences in hardness of woods.

Additional reading

Dunkin, M. J. and Biddle, B. J. (1974) *A Study of Teaching*, Holt, Rinehart and Winston, New York. Ch. 6: Management and control, and Ch. 7: The classroom as a social system (pp. 134–230).

Greig, T. O. and Brown, J. C. (1975) *Activity Methods in the Middle Years*, Longman, London.

Perrott, E., Hind, R., Salfield, P. and Woolerton, A. (1977) *Planning Independent Studies*, Guild Sound and Vision Ltd, Peterborough, 2 vols and 5 videotapes or films. This is a self-instructional microteaching course with a workbook and five videotapes or films showing experienced teachers demonstrating different stages in planning independent studies.

Plowden, Lady B. et al. (1967) *Children and their Primary Schools*, a report of the Central Advisory Council for Education, HMSO, London.

Walton, J. and Ruck, J. (eds.) (1975) *Resources and Resource Centres*, Ward Lock Educational, London.

Taba, H. (1962) *Curriculum Development: Theory and Practice*, Harcourt Brace and World, New York, Ch. 24.

Chapter 8

Techniques for the recording of classroom teaching events

Because there is so much to observe in a full-size class, it is impossible for the casual observer to sort out and isolate specific acts that sometimes hold the key to solving teaching problems or changing classroom behaviour.

Observation systems for specific concerns have been developed, and experience will suggest which one is the most appropriate for use in given circumstances.

The observation techniques described in this chapter provide a means of recording and analysing specific teaching events in a full-size class. Most of them are easily understood and can be used effectively after a little practice. They may be used by an observer, recording with pencil and paper, during a classroom session, or by the teacher himself using an audio- or video-recording of the classroom session from which to record.

Selective verbatim

As the term suggests, when using the selective verbatim technique the observer (or teacher using an audio-recording of his own lesson), makes a written record of exactly what is said: that is a verbatim transcript. Not all verbal events are written down, however; in this sense the verbatim record is 'selective'. First of all the verbal reactions to be analysed are identified. These are interactions that reflect effective or ineffective teaching, such as teacher questions, pupils' responses, teacher's responses, teacher's directions. The actual words used are recorded and then the data are analysed. Selective verbatim has a number of obvious advantages as an observation technique.

(a) It focuses the teacher's attention on what he actually says to pupils or on what the pupils say to him. All other classroom events are screened out for the time being.

(b) It allows the teacher to concentrate on one aspect of his teaching behaviour at a time. This makes change more manageable and encourages further change.

(c) It provides an objective non-interpretive record of teaching behaviour, which can be analysed after the lesson is over. In 'live' classroom teaching verbal events occur rapidly and are forgotten before the teacher can reflect on their effectiveness.

Unless classroom verbal interaction is mechanically recorded it is often difficult for an observer to keep up with verbal interaction by written recording. One mechanical recording of all verbal interaction can provide material for several selective verbatim transcripts, e.g. of teacher's questions, teacher's directions and teacher's responses.

Exercise 8.1

From an audio-recording of one of your discussion lessons, record and analyse the questions you asked.

It is not unusual for a teacher to use on average two questions every minute during a half-hour discussion period (Schreiber 1967). As a rule only a small proportion of these are planned. Many teachers have never listened to and systematically analysed the questions they use in class.

Data collection

From an audio-recording of a discussion with your class, record verbatim all the questions you asked. The resulting data will permit a comparison between 'what you wanted' and 'what you asked for'. If it will take too long to record all your questions, observe time samples of the lesson, e.g. the first five minutes, five minutes in the middle of the lesson and then five minutes at the end.

Data analysis

Useful questions to ask when you analyse your questions are:

(a) What was the cognitive level of the questions? Did they demand a recall of facts, higher cognitive thinking or both? (See Ch. 4 p. 48.)

(b) Was any particular pattern of questioning revealed, e.g. questions that produced one-word answers?

(c) How often did you use questions that begin with 'What', or started with the same phrase such as 'Do you think ...?'

(d) What was the relation between the objectives of the lesson and the questions asked?

(e) Was the vocabulary you used suitable for the pupils' verbal ability?

(f) Were probing questions used? (See Ch. 5 p. 65.)

(g) Did you avoid multiple questions? The practice of asking several questions in a row without giving the pupils the opportunity to respond can easily be spotted when using selective verbatim. Sometimes the question is simply rephrased and repeated, but it is a practice which does not encourage pupils to listen carefully to questions and is to be avoided. It can be confusing to pupils if a variety of phrasings and ideas are used before hitting on the question you want to ask. If you make use of several multiple questions, avoid 'thinking on your feet' and prepare questions in advance of the lesson. The results of your analysis should provide information which can be of use in modifying your questioning style.

Exercise 8.2

From an audio-recording of one of your discussion lessons record and analyse the verbal responses which you gave to pupils.

The verbal responses or feedback which the teacher gives to pupils has an effect on the learning process. We all need feedback to know how well we are performing any new skill. Praise or negative remarks, which are a form of feedback, also affect behaviour, especially motivation to learn.

Research studies have shown that teachers' verbal responses tend to be restricted, only a few kinds of response being used regularly. Zahorik (1967) and Flanders (1970), have found that the most common form of feedback to pupils was simply to repeat the pupil's answer to a question. In their review of research on teachers' use of criticism, Rosenshine and Furst (1971) found evidence that teachers who use extreme amounts of criticism usually have classes that achieve less in most subject areas. On the other hand, praise has been shown to have a positive effect (Ch. 6).

Data collection

From an audio-recording of a discussion with your class, record verbatim all the responses which you made to pupils' answers or questions. You might also find it useful to record the immediately preceding pupil's remark which prompted the response. If it will take too long to record all your responses, observe time samples of the lesson, e.g. ten minutes in the middle of the lesson and five minutes at the end. Alternatively, you might restrict your recording to responses giving praise and criticism. Other responses can be recorded as r.ig. (response ignored). You might find it useful to record the immediately· preceding pupil's remark or action which elicited a response.

Data analysis

You can examine this selective verbatim from several perspectives.

(a) The simplest analysis is that of the *amount* of feedback, or the frequency with which the teacher responds to pupils. Teachers who provide very little feedback use a very directive style of teaching. Their primary concern is to impart knowledge with too little concern about their pupils' reaction to it. Other teachers make extensive use of feedback. They tend to be more responsive to their pupils and to encourage teacher–pupil interaction.

(b) Another useful type of analysis is to look at the kinds of responses made. Flanders (1970) found that teachers mostly provide feedback on pupils' ideas by acknowledging them. This might take the form of 'yes', 'all right' or repeating the pupil's idea virtually verbatim. Flanders has shown that the pupils' ideas can be acknowledged and used more effectively by either *modifying* the idea, i.e. rephrasing it in the teachers' own words; *applying* the idea by using it to reach an inference or take the next step in solving a problem; comparing the idea with other ideas expressed earlier by the pupils or the teacher; or *summarizing* what was said by one or several pupils.

(c) Verbal feedback can also be analysed for use of praise and criticism. When a teacher's response contains a value judgement such as 'yes, that's good', but does not indicate the criteria on which the response is based, it is not as helpful to the pupil as when the initial response is followed by an explanation of the praise or criticism (Flanders 1970), e.g. 'good, that answer was the result of very careful observation'. A rapid inspection of a selective verbatim will help you to see whether you use simple or elaborated responses.

(d) Other points worth consideration are: Were your responses enthusiastic, automatic or hostile? Were pupils' names used?

Exercise 8.3

Teacher's directions and structuring statements

Teachers frequently use statements to give directions and structure the learning situation, e.g, telling pupils how to carry out an assignment, or what to do in preparation for an examination.

Research studies consistently have found that higher levels of pupils' achievement are associated with teachers who make use of structuring statements (Rosenshine and Furst 1973). Similar research has been done on the effects of teacher directions. Clearly, teachers who give vague, ambiguous directions will confuse pupils and interfere with their learning.

Data collection

From an audio-recording of an entire lesson make a selective verbatim of each set of directions and any structuring statements. The majority of such statements usually occur at the beginning and the end of a lesson.

Data analysis

Observe the amount, variety and specificity of directions and structuring statements. Also evaluate the clarity of your structuring statements.

Directions and structuring statements which you might expect to find in your selective verbatim are:

(a) An overview of the lesson.
(b) The objectives and purpose of the lesson.
(c) Cueing remarks that focus on key points in the lesson.
(d) A summary of what was covered in the lesson.
(e) Statements relating the lesson to a wider context, e.g. curriculum content or events outside the classroom.
(f) Directions concerning what pupils are to do when the lesson is in progress or when the lesson is completed.
(g) Reinforcement of directions and structuring statements by repeating them in another format, e.g. by writing them on the blackboard, or by means of a handout.

Records based on seating charts

Some techniques for observing the behaviour of teacher and pupils make use of seating charts. These techniques have the advantage that as teachers commonly use seating charts for other purposes, they usually find it easy to interpret data presented in this manner. They may be used to record a variety of data, e.g. pupils' level of attentiveness (the 'at-task' technique), or how a teacher distributes his time among the pupils in his class (by recording teacher and pupil movements).

The 'at-task' technique

The 'at-task' technique was originally developed by McGraw (1966). He devised a system which used a remotely controlled 35 mm camera for classroom observation. From the front corner of the room a camera with a wide-angle lens took a picture of the class every ninety seconds. When the photographs were developed and enlarged, the observer was provided with a set of pictures of the classroom taken over a given time. The data obtained were valuable for the teacher in understanding individual pupils, as it showed some concentrating on the required task throughout while others neglected the task to talk to neighbours or day-dream.

Although valuable, the method of data collection proved to be expensive and time consuming. Therefore, experiments were conducted using alternative methods. Ultimately the paper and pencil technique known as 'at-task' was developed (see Fig. 8.1). These records must be made by an observer when a class is in progress or can be made by the teacher himself from a video-recording of the entire class.

Research studies have demonstrated that the pupils' at-task behaviour is an important factor in learning (Rosenshine and Berliner 1978). It seems obvious that the more a pupil attends to the tasks presented by the teacher, the more he is likely to learn. Although this is not always the case, nevertheless if pupils are at task, one can suppose with confidence that some learning is taking place.

Exercise 8.4

Assess the extent to which your pupils are engaged in expected behaviour or at task. Arrange either for a video-recording to be made of

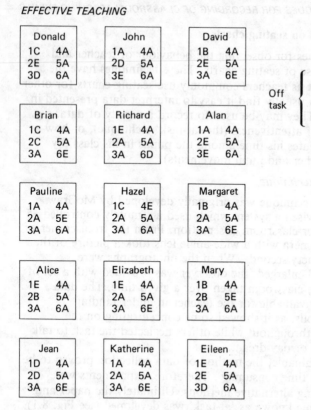

Donald	**John**	**David**
1C 4A	1A 4A	1B 4A
2E 5A	2D 5A	2E 5A
3D 6A	3E 6A	3A 6E

Categories

Off task

A At task
B Idle
C Schoolwork not required
D Out of seat
E Talking to other pupils.

Brian	**Richard**	**Alan**
1C 4A	1E 4A	1A 4A
2C 5A	2A 5A	2E 5A
3A 6E	3A 6D	3E 6A

Pauline	**Hazel**	**Margaret**
1A 4A	1C 4E	1B 4A
2A 5E	2A 5A	2A 5A
3A 6A	3A 6A	3A 6E

Alice	**Elizabeth**	**Mary**
1E 4A	1E 4A	1B 4A
2B 5A	2A 5A	2B 5E
3A 6A	3A 6E	3A 6A

Jean	**Katherine**	**Eileen**
1D 4A	1A 4A	1E 4A
2D 5A	2A 5A	2E 5A
3A 6E	3A 6E	3D 6A

Summary of observations

At-task categories	Times of observation						Total	%
	9.35	9.40	9.45	9.50	9.55	10.00		
At task — A	4	6	11	14	13	8	56	62
Off task								
Idle — B	3	2	0	0	0	0	5	6
Schoolwork not requested — C	3	1	0	0	0	0	4	4
Out of seat — D	1	2	2	0	0	1	6	7
Talking to others — E	4	4	2	1	2	6	19	21

Note: Ten minutes had elapsed before most of the class had settled down to the assigned task. Almost half the class had completed the task before the end of the lesson and were not given another task in which to engage while the rest completed the task.

Fig. 8.1 Seating chart showing 'at-task' data for a geography lesson in which pupils were required to draw a map showing the distribution of coalfields.

the whole class during an entire lesson or for an observer to record at-task data on a seating chart over this period. If an observer is employed it is important that he be supplied with notes for the aims and methods to be employed in the lesson.

Classrooms where one task is expected of all pupils usually present no problem. But in classrooms where pupils are to be free to engage in a variety of tasks it may be necessary to limit observation and recording to one group or section of the classroom.

Data collection

1. Construct a seating chart of your group and indicate name and sex of pupils on it.
2. Devise a set of symbols to represent a range of at-task categories, e.g.
   A at task;
   B idle or off task;
   C schoolwork not requested by teacher or off task;
   D out of seat or off task;
   E talking to other pupils or off task.
3. Define A for the lesson being observed.
4. Systematically examine the behaviour of each pupil for a few seconds in order to determine whether the pupil is engaged on the task required. Indicate the behaviour observed by the use of the symbols above, together with a number 1 indicating first observation (see Fig. 8.1).
5. Repeat (4) at convenient time intervals until you have several numbered and lettered observations noted in each box (see Fig. 8.1), e.g. 1C, 2A, 3A, 4A, 5E. It is important to remember that you are making assessments of appropriate behaviour, for instance a pupil may be out of his seat conferring with another pupil. Providing this is an allowed behaviour and the pupil is discussing the task, it is appropriate behaviour A, not D or E. Avoid adding more than five categories as this complicates observation.

Therefore, the data are more useful in showing general patterns than in individual observations. If an observer is used it is important that the feedback session is held as soon as possible, while the lesson is fresh in the teacher's mind.

Data analysis

Before at-task behaviour can be adequately analysed, make a summary of the observations recorded on the seating chart (see Fig. 8.1). This will allow you to see at a glance how many pupils were engaged in each category of behaviour, either at a particular point in the lesson or summed across all the time samples.

The verbal flow technique

Another aspect of classroom behaviour which can be recorded on a seating chart is verbal flow. This is primarily a technique which shows who is talking to whom. It can be used to record and analyse classroom discussions. Whereas selective verbation is concerned with the content of verbal behaviour, verbal flow identifies the initiators and recipients of verbal communication and the kind of communication in which they are engaged. Research has identified forms of bias in the verbal behaviour of teachers. For instance Dunkin and Biddle (1974) have shown that the majority of both emitters and targets of verbal behaviour are located in the front or centre of the class. It has also identified a number of factors related to differences in behaviour of pupils. Gall and Gall (1976) in a review of research on discussion groups found that black pupils tend to participate less in discussion than white pupils, and younger pupils tend to participate less than older pupils. Also, males tend to initiate more verbal acts than do females. This sex difference has been found to occur even among young children.

The verbal flow technique can help the teacher to discover (a) biases in your own verbal behaviour, and (b) differences between the verbal participation of different pupils.

The use of verbal flow techniques are particularly appropriate when a lesson involves discussion, question and answer sequences and other methods requiring verbal interchange between the teacher and the class.

Exercise 8.5

Record and analyse classroom verbal flow in one of your discussion lessons. Arrange for either a video-recording of the entire lesson to be made from which data can be subsequently recorded, or for an observer to record verbal flow data on a seating chart during the lesson. The advantage of the video-recording is that it can be stopped and started and you can record the data either by yourself or together with a colleague or supervisor for subsequent discussion. Alternatively, record verbal flow in someone else's lesson.

Data collection

1. Construct a seating chart of your group and indicate the name or sex of the pupils on it.
2. Select an appropriate set of symbols.
3. Using an appropriate symbol, indicate on the seating chart each time someone speaks. Arrows are used to indicate the flow of interaction. The base of the arrow indicates the person who initiates the verbal interaction. When the teacher initiates a verbal interaction with a pupil the arrow is placed in the pupil's box with the base of the arrow coming from the direction of the teacher (see Fig. 8.2). Repeated interactions of the same kind instead of being indicated by additional arrows are shown by cross-bars on the original arrows, i.e.

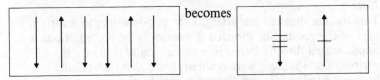

thus keeping the record visually simple. Analysis of these data indicates that the teacher initiated this interaction and directed four comments in all to the pupil, while the pupil directed two comments back to the teacher. The standard verbal flow can be elaborated by using additional categories of observation as appropriate. For example:

⟶   + teacher's praise or encouragement

⟶   − teacher's criticism

⟶   ? teacher's question

⟵   ✓ pupil volunteered correct or relevant response

⟵   × pupil volunteered incorrect or irrelevant response

⟵   ? pupil's question

Data analysis

Verbal flow data can be analysed in numerous ways. For
instance:

(i)   Seat location preferences
      Have you directed more of your attention to pupils seated
      in a certain part of the room?
(ii) Pupil preference
      Did you react equally with boys and girls?
(iii) Verbal behaviour preference
      Did you use more positive than negative responses?

Figure 8.2, p. 181 shows a verbal flow chart made of a class
discussion at the end of a junior science class.

Note

This teacher directed her attention to pupils sitting in a certain
part of the room. She directed the majority of her questions to
pupils seated directly in her line of sight, and those on the
periphery of the class were ignored. Note also that talking
between pupils while the discussion was in progress occurred on
the periphery of the class.

It is also shown that this teacher directed the majority of her
questions to the boys. There are 14 girls and 11 boys in this
class; 7 boys were questioned by the teacher and only 5 girls.
Also, of the positive responses given by the teacher seven were
directed to boys and four to girls; while the only negative
responses were directed to girls. Nine of the 14 girls and 4 of the
11 boys did not participate in the discussion. These data suggest
a sex bias favouring boys. Also 2 pupils, 1 boy and 1 girl,
dominated the participation. (Additional boxes were necessary to
contain their data.)

Movement patterns

Another use of seating charts is to record the movements of
teacher and pupils during a class lesson. Many teaching
situations, e.g. most primary school classrooms, together with
the science laboratory and other classrooms in secondary
schools, especially those where pupils are involved in practical
work or small-group work, e.g. domestic science, art and crafts,
etc., require teachers to make decisions about where to position
themselves and resources in the classroom. The nature of the
teacher's and pupils' movement patterns can have an important

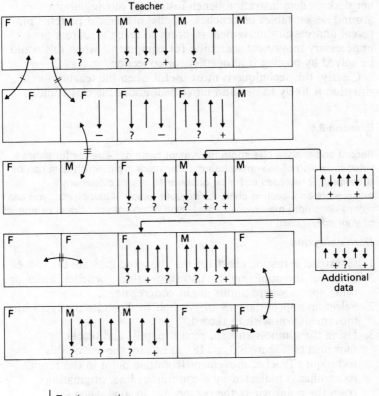

Teacher

↓ Teacher question
?

↑ Pupil response

↓ Teacher's positive response
+

↓ Teacher's negative response
−

Fig. 8.2 Verbal flow chart of class discussion in a junior science class.

effect on classroom control. Records of teacher's movement patterns often show a consistent bias which can create difficulties, e.g. the teacher who prefers to remain behind his or her desk or demonstration bench instead of moving about around desks, tables or benches. Pupils' movement patterns may reveal unnecessary movement in order to reach resources or unnecessary movement searching for equipment, when this could be solved by placing it altogether for collection.

Clearly, this technique is most useful when the teaching situation is likely to demand movement about the classroom.

Exercise 8.6

Record and analyse classroom movement patterns. Arrange for either a video-recording of the entire lesson to be made from which data can be subsequently recorded or for an observer to record classroom movements on a seating chart during your lesson. Alternatively, you can record classroom movement in the lesson of one of your tutors or one of your colleagues.

Data collection

1. Construct a seating chart for the class and indicate the names or sex of the pupils on it. Also show tables, benches, aisles or other spaces where pupils might congregate.
2. Select an appropriate set of symbols to illustrate the types of movement you wish to record.
3. Using the symbols chosen, record pupils' and teacher's movements. Figure 8.3, p. 183 illustrates the use of this technique. Teacher movement from one point in the room to another is indicated by a continuous line, originating from the point where the person was located when the observation was made. Stopping points are represented by a circled number.
4. Coloured pencils may be used to record movement at different points in the lesson, e.g. the first ten minutes could be recorded in red, the second ten minutes in green, etc. If there is too much movement to record all of it, concentrate your attention on specific pupils.

Data analysis

Figure 8.3 shows a middle school science class where pupils were working in pairs on an experiment. The teacher started the lesson standing behind the demonstration bench. She next moved to pupil 1 and then proceeded to pupil 11, the arrows indicating the direction of her progress. When analysing classroom movement

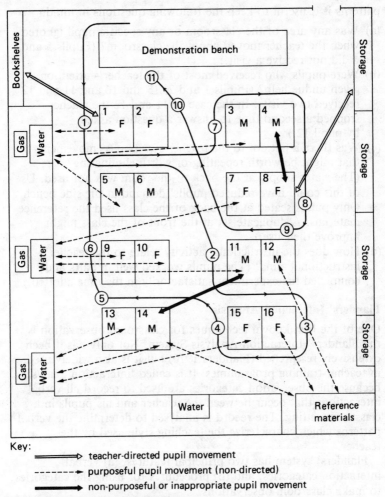

Key:

⟹ teacher-directed pupil movement

- - - → purposeful pupil movement (non-directed)

➡ non-purposeful or inappropriate pupil movement

→ teacher movement.

① Pupil-teacher conference

Fig. 8.3 Observation of physical movement data in a middle school science class.

patterns it is useful to keep the following questions in mind:

(a) Was any area of the classroom or any specific pupil ignored when the teacher moved about the classroom? (Pupils 5 and 6 did not receive a visit.)

(b) Were pupils who received most of the teacher's attention given undue help? (Pupils 1 and 2, 15 and 16 and 11 and 12 received two visits. In the case of 11 and 12 the teacher stopped a second time to answer a question asked by pupil 12.)

(c) Was there a pattern to the teacher's or pupils' movements that might be worth repeating or worth eliminating? (The water supply at the back of the room was not used. Use of this could have reduced pupils' demand at the side bench. Only pupils seated at the back of the class used the reference materials. A duplicate set at the front of the class might improve their use.)

(d) How does the instructional activity relate to the teacher's instructional aims? (The pupils worked well in pairs and completed the experiment satisfactorily in the time allotted.)

Flanders' Interaction Analysis

One of the best known techniques for classroom observation is the Flanders' Interaction Analysis System. Not only has it been extensively researched (Flanders 1970) but it is also widely used in teacher-training programmes. It is called 'interaction analysis' because the observation categories are used to record all verbal interactions that occur between the teacher and his pupils in a classroom setting. The record is analysed to determine the verbal patterns which characterize the teaching style used by the teacher.

Flanders' system has two principal features, (a) verbal interaction categories, and (b) procedures for using the categories to make classroom observations.

Flanders' verbal interaction categories

These verbal interaction categories are shown in Table 8.1, p. 185. With the exception of category 10 (silence or confusion) all categories describe a specific type of verbal behaviour. Any verbal statement made by a teacher can be classified into one of the nine categories. This is true irrespective of the subject being taught or the level to which it is taught. It cannot be used to analyse classroom activities involving no interaction between the teacher and his pupils, for instance, when the class is engaged in independent work, watching a film or listening to a broadcast.

The critical distinction in Flander's system is between response and initiation. Some of the categories of verbal behaviour are either responses the teacher makes to pupils' comments (categories 1, 2 and 3) or responses a pupil might make to a teacher comment (category 8). Others are intended to initiate communication, with either pupil (category 9) or teacher (categories 5, 6 and 7) playing the role of initiator. Categories 4

Table 8.1 Interaction Analysis Categories* (Flanders 1970)

Teacher talk	Response	1. *Accepts feeling.* Accepts and clarifies an attitude or the feeling tone of a student in a non-threatening manner. Feelings may be positive or negative. Predicting and recalling feeling are included
		2. *Praises or encourages.* Praises or encourages students; says 'um hum' or 'go on'; makes jokes that release tension, but not at the expense of the student
		3. *Accepts or uses ideas of students.* Acknowledges student talk. Clarifies, builds on or asks questions based on student ideas
	Initiation	4. *Asks questions.* Asks questions about content or procedure, based on teacher ideas; with intent that a student will answer
		5. *Lectures.* Offers facts or opinions about content or procedures; expresses his own ideas, gives his own explanation or cites an authority other than student
		6. *Gives directions.* Gives directions, commands or orders with which a student is expected to comply
		7. *Criticizes student or justifies authority.* Makes statements intended to change student behaviour from non-acceptable to acceptable patterns; arbitrarily corrects student answers; bawls someone out. Or states why the teacher is doing what he is doing; uses extreme self-reference

	Response	8.	*Student talk – response.* Student talk in response to a teacher contact that structures or limits the situation. Freedom to express own ideas is limited
Student talk	Initiation	9.	*Student talk – initiation.* Student initiates or expresses his own ideas, either spontaneously or in response to the teacher's solicitation. Freedom to develop opinions and a line of thought; going beyond existing structure
Silence		10.	*Silence or confusion.* Pauses, short periods of silence and periods of confusion in which communication cannot be understood by the observer

* Based on Flanders, N. A., *Analyzing Teaching Behaviour*, 1970. No scale is implied by these numbers. Each number is classificatory; it designates a particular kind of communication event. To write these numbers down during observation is to enumerate, not to judge a position on a scale.

and 10 are neutral, reflecting neither response nor initiation.

To initiate is to take the lead – to give directions, express one's will or needs, to introduce new ideas or act independently.

To respond is to react to the ideas or demands someone else has initiated by amplifying on or conforming to them.

An important dimension of the interaction between you and your pupils which Flanders' Interaction Analysis will help you analyse is the balance of initiation and response between teacher and pupils in the classroom. In general, there is a complementary relationship between teacher initiation and response and pupil response and initiation. Teacher initiation generally stimulates pupil response and teacher response stimulates pupil initiation.

Research studies undertaken with student teachers have indicated that learning to use interaction analysis results in more 'indirect' or responsive teaching style (Hough and Amidon 1964), the implication being that by the teacher categorizing how he and his pupils interact results in an awareness which can lead to change. Research also suggests that the use of such a style is associated with more positive pupil attitudes and higher pupil achievement (Flanders 1970).

An 'indirect' or responsive style of teaching is associated with affective behaviours such as accepting feeling, praising and acknowledging students' ideas. When a teacher initiates all the verbal exchanges he is said to be using a 'direct' style of teaching. According to this category system asking questions is neutral – neither direct nor indirect. It is thought that a teacher's use of an indirect style of teaching (categories 1, 2 and 3) encourages pupils to increase the frequency with which they offer their own ideas and opinions (category 9). In contrast, a teacher's use of a directive style (categories 5, 6 and 7) is thought to channel pupils' ideas and behaviour to meet the teacher's expectations (category 8).

Research also suggests that the use of such a style is associated with more positive pupil attitudes and higher pupil achievement (Flanders 1970). But this does not mean that a direct style is necessarily poor teaching. Flanders suggests that there are times when the teacher needs to be direct, for example, when presenting new content to pupils and giving directions. But even direct teaching presents opportunities for some indirect verbal behaviours. For instance, the teacher may be giving an extended series of directions to the class for carrying out an experiment. While doing this he might pause to praise or encourage pupils for their efforts and success in following his instructions (category 2), i.e. the teacher intersperses direct teaching with indirect teaching behaviours. Likewise, direct teaching behaviours are often interspersed into a predominant indirect pupil-centred lesson. In other words, a flexible use of appropriate behaviours in both indirect and direct teaching behaviours is the aim.

Procedures for using Flanders' categories

Interaction is coded on a timetable display, which is designed so that you can check categories of interaction as quickly as they occur when you are listening to an audiotape of your lesson or observing someone else's lesson. It is also designed for quick interpretation of verbal patterns. Figure 8.4 presents several examples of timelines, which have been used to record verbal interaction in a classroom, using Flanders' categories. Each square represents a three-second interval and each timeline has thirty squares for recording thirty discrete observations. Since an observation is made every three seconds one timeline covers one and a half minutes of classroom interaction.

187

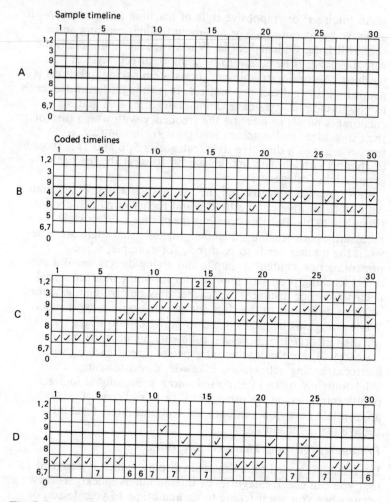

Fig. 8.4 Timelines.

Each row represents one or two interaction categories, with the middle row for category 4 – teacher questions. Categories reflecting an indirect teaching style (1, 2 and 3) are above the middle row as is the category reflecting open pupil-initiated responses (category 9). Categories that indicate a direct teaching style (5, 6 and 7) are below the middle row, as is the category for structured pupil responses (category 8). Category 10 is not represented by a row. Tallies for this category are made below the timeline. Where two categories share the same row, they may be differentiated by using the number instead of a simple tally to record incidence (see Fig. 8.4).

When the majority of tallies are above the middle row an indirect teaching style is indicated. When the majority of tallies are below the middle row a direct teaching style is indicated.

Decoding a timeline

Timeline A (Fig. 8.4) is a sample on which an interaction has not been completed.

Timeline B is characterized by alternating 4s and 8s, suggesting a rapid question-and-answer interaction focused on the recall of facts.

Timeline C suggests a more indirect interaction. The teacher begins by giving information on a specific topic and then invites the pupils to offer their own ideas on the topic. Each pupil's response is acknowledged or praised.

Timeline D suggests that the teacher is probably criticizing pupils and/or justifying authority, and there is no indication that the pupils are given reasons for the teacher's remarks. Notice that none of the 7s are followed or preceded by 1, 2 or 3, indicating that the teacher is not coupling criticism with acceptance.

Exercise 8.7

Prepare three timelines. Code three one and a half minute samples from an audio-recording of one of your microlessons. Remember you will need a stop-watch to time yourself. Space your samples so that one is taken at the beginning, one in the middle and one at the end of your microlesson. Decode or analyse.

Additional reading

Rosenshine, Barak, *Teaching Behaviours and Student Achievement*, National Foundation for Educational Research, Slough, Bucks.

Flanders, N. et al. (1974) *Interaction Analysis: A Mini-course*. Available from Paul S. Amidon and Associates, Inc., 4329 Nicollet Avenue South, Minneapolis, MN 55409.

This course which consists of two volumes, a handbook and workbook, together with an audio-cassette is a self-instructional mini-course developed by Flanders and his colleagues at the Teacher

Educational Division of the Far West Laboratory, San Francisco, to help teachers analyse their own teacher.

References

Abercrombie, M. L. J. (1971) *Aims and Techniques of Group Teaching*, Society for Research into Higher Education, University of Surrey, England.

Allen, D. W., Fortune, J. C. and Cooper J. M. (1968) The Stanford Summer Micro-Teaching Clinic, in *Microteaching: a description*, School of Education, Stanford University (mimeo).

Allen, D. W. and Ryan, K. (1969) *Microteaching*, Addison-Wesley, Reading, MA.

Amidon, E. J. and Hough, J. B. (eds) (1967) *Interaction Analysis: Theory, Research and Applications*, Addison-Wesley, Reading, M.A.

Anderson, R. C. and Ausubel, D. P. (1965) *Readings in the Psychology Cognition*, Holt, Rinehart and Winston, New York.

Argyle, M. (1970) *Social Interaction*, Methuen, London.

Ausubel, D. P. (1965) Introduction, in Anderson, R. C. and Ausubel, D. P. (eds), *Readings in the Psychology of Cognition*, Holt, Rinehart and Winston, New York.

Bellack, A. A., Kliebard, H. M., Hyman, R. T. and Smith, F. L. (1966) *The Language of the Classroom*, Teachers' College Press, Columbia Univ., New York.

Bennett, N. (1976) *Teaching Styles and Pupil Progress*, Open Books, London.

Berliner, D. C. and Tickenoff, W. J. (1976) The California Beginning Teacher Evaluation Study: overview of the Ethnographic Study, *Journal of Teacher Education*, **27**, 24–30.

Bloom, B. S. (1956) *Taxonomy of Educational Objectives*, Handbook 1 (Cognitive Domain), Longman, London.

Borg, W. R., Kelly, M. L., Langer, P. and Gall, M. (1970) *The Minicourse: A Microteaching Approach to Teacher Training*, Macmillan, London.

Bruner, J. S. (1960) *The Process of Education*, Harvard Univ., Cambridge, Mass. pp. 17–32.

DeCecco, J. P. (1968) *The Psychology of Learning and Instruction*, Prentice-Hall, Englewood Cliffs, New Jersey.

Dunkin, M. J. and Biddle, B. J. (1974) *The Study of Teaching*, Holt, Rinehart and Winston, New York and London, p. 226.

Flanders, N. A. (1970) *Analyzing Teaching Behaviour*, Addison-Wesley, Reading, MA.

Flanders, N. A. and Simon, A. (1969) Teacher effectiveness, in Ebel, R. L. (ed.), *Encyclopaedia of Educational Research*, Macmillan, New York.

Floyd, W. D. (1966) An analysis of the oral questioning activity in selected Colorado primary classrooms, Ph.D. diss. Columbia Univ., New York.

Gage, N. L. (ed.) (1976) *The Psychology of Teaching Methods*, *75th Yearbook of the National Society for the Study of Education*, University of Chicago Press, Chicago, Illinois.

Gage, N. L. and Berliner, D. C. (1975) *Educational Psychology*, Rand McNally, Chicago.

Gagné, R. M. (1965) *The Conditions of Learning*, Holt, Rinehart and Winston, New York, pp. 172–204.

Gall, M. D. and Gall, J. P. (1976) The discussion method, in Gage, N. L. (ed.), *The Psychology of Teaching Methods*, *75th Yearbook of the National Society for the Study of Education*, University of Chicago Press, Chicago, Illinois.

Groisser, P. (1964) *How to Use the Fine Art of Questioning*, Teachers' Practical Press, New York.

Hall, E. T. (1966) *The Hidden Dimensions*, Doubleday, New York.

Hough, J. B. and Amidon, E. J. (1964) An experiment in pre-service teacher education, paper presented at a meeting of the American Educational Research Association, Chicago, Illinois.

Hunkins, F. P. (1966) Using questions to foster pupils' thinking, *Education*, **87**, 83–87.

Hunkins, F. P. (1972) *Questioning Strategies and Techniques*, Allyn and Bacon, Boston.

Kounin, J. (1970) *Discipline and Group Management*, Holt, Rinehart and Winston, New York.

Krasner, L. (1958) Studies of the conditioning of verbal behaviour, *Psychological Bulletin*, **55**, 148–71.

McGraw, F. (1966) *The Use of 35 mm Time-lapse Photography as a Feedback and Observation Instrument* in *Teacher Instrument*, University Microfilms, 66–2516, Ann Arbor, MI.

McKeachie, W. J. (1963) Research on teaching at the college and university level, in Gage, N. L. (ed.), *Handbook of Research on Teaching*, Rand McNally, Chicago.

Martorella, P. H. (1972) *Concept Learning: Designs for Instruction*, International Textbook, New York.

Mehrabian, A. and Wiener, A. (1966) Non-immediacy between communication and object of communication in a verbal message, *Journal of Consulting Psychology*, **30**. American Psychological Association, Washington.

Millenson, J. R. (1967) *Principles of Behaviour Analysis*, Macmillan, New York.

Moyer, J. R. (1966) An exploratory study of questioning in the instructional processes in selected elementary schools, Ph.D. diss. Columbia Univ., New York.

OECD Report (1975) *The International Transfer of Microteaching Programmes for Teacher Education*, Centre for Educational Research and Innovation, Paris.

Perrott, E. (1977) *Microteaching in Higher Education: Research, Development and Practice* (monograph), Society for Research into Higher Education, Univ. of Surrey, Guildford.

Perrott, E., Applebee, A. N., Heap, B. and Watson, E. (1975a) Changes in teaching behaviour after completing a self-instructional microteaching course, *Programmed Learning and Educational Technology*, **12** (16), 348–62.

Perrott, E., Applebee, A. N., Watson, E. and Heap, B. (1975b) *A Self-instructional Microteaching Course on 'Effective Questioning'*, Guild Sound & Vision, Peterborough (3 vols and 5 videotapes or film programmes).

Perrott, E., Hind, R., Salfield, P. and Woolerton, A. (1977) *A Self-instructional Microteaching Course on 'Planning Independent Studies'*, Guild Sound & Vision, Peterborough (2 vols and 5 videotape programmes).

Rosenshine, B. (1970) Enthusiastic teaching: a research review, *School Rev.*, **78**, 499–514, reprinted in Morrison, A. and McIntyre, D. (eds.) (1972) *The Social Psychology of Teaching*, Penguin, Harmondsworth.

Rosenshine, B. (1971) *Teaching Behaviours and Student Achievement*, IEA Studies, No. 1, National Foundation of Educational Research, Slough.

Rosenshine, B. and Berliner, D. (1978) Academic engaged time, *British Journal of Teacher Education*, **4**, 3–16.

Rosenshine, B. and Furst, A. F. (1971) Research on teacher performance criteria, in Smith, B. O. (ed.), *Research in Teacher Education: A Symposium*, Prentice-Hall, Englewood Cliffs, New Jersey.

Rosenshine, B. and Furst, A. F. (1973) The use of direct observation to study teaching, in Travers, R.M. (ed.), *Second Handbook of Research on Teaching*, Rand McNally, Chicago.

193

Ryan, D. (1960) *Characteristics of Teachers*, American Council on Education, Washington DC.

Schreiber, J. E. (1967) Teachers' questions – asking techniques in social studies, Ph.D. diss. Univ. of Iowa.

Smith, B. O. (1969) *Teachers for the Real World*, American Association of Colleges for Teacher Education, Washington DC, p. 122.

Stevens, R. (1912) The question as a measure of efficiency in instruction, *Teachers' College Contributions to Education*, No. 48, Teachers' College Press, Columbia Univ., New York.

Taba, H., Levine, S. and Elzey, F. F. (1964) *Thinking in Elementary Schoolchildren*, US Office of Education, Co-operative Research Project, No. 1574, San Francisco State College, San Francisco.

Zahorik, J. A. (1967) Classroom feedback behaviour of teachers, *Journal of Educational Research*, **62**, 147–50.

Index